MAN'S DESTINY IN ETERNITY

MAN'S DESTINY IN ETERNITY

The Garvin Lectures

Arthur H. Compton · Jacques Maritain

Maude Royden · Hornell Hart

Reinhold Niebuhr · William Ernest Hocking

Charles E. Park . Willard L. Sperry

F. S. C. Northrop

Essay Index Reprint Series

BOOKS FOR LIBRARIES PRESS

FREEPORT, NEW YORK

Reprinted 1970 by arrangement with Beacon Press

INTERNATIONAL STANDARD BOOK NUMBER:

0-8369-1762-6

LIBRARY OF CONGRESS CATALOG CARD NUMBER:

75-117821

PRINTED IN THE UNITED STATES OF AMERICA

PREFACE

M. T. Garvin was a successful retail merchant who lived in Lancaster, Pennsylvania. He died on August 18, 1936.

In his will he provided for an endowment of $10,000 for the delivery of lectures on the subjects " The Idea of God as Affected by Modern Knowledge " and " The Immortality of Man." The exact language of the bequest, which was drafted by Mr. Garvin in longhand and incorporated without substantial change in the text of the will, is as follows:

Ten thousand dollars ($10,000.00) to be retained by my said executors, as trustees, to hold in trust and invest the same, the income therefrom to be used in the following manner.

After an active life among my fellow men I am convinced by experience and observation that the highest inspiration comes to man through an abiding faith in the Eternal Spirit, the Creator of the Universe and the source of the laws which govern it. I am also convinced that man needs as a foundation for daily life the knowledge and conviction that he is destined to immortal life, and that intellectual and spiritual growth go on forever. That these convictions are not shared by all men I am aware, and, in order that they may more widely prevail, my said executors, as trustees, shall use the income from said sum of $10,000.00 for the purpose of providing lectures on the subjects " The Idea of God as Affected by Modern Knowledge " and " The Immortality of Man." These lectures shall be given alternately one each year by clergymen or laymen of standing in the world of scholarship, without regard to denomination or profession. One lecture shall be delivered each calendar year, and the lecturer shall be selected by a committee consisting of my executors and the ministers of the Church of Our Father, Unitarian, Lancaster, Pennsylvania, the First Unitarian Church of Philadelphia, Pa., and the Unitarian Church of Germantown, Pa. Said lectures are to be given in the Church of Our Father, Unitarian, Lancaster, Pennsylvania. Three-fourths of the income of the fund hereby set apart is to be given to the lecturer, and the other one-fourth shall be used for publicity, incidental expenses, and the publication of said lectures for

v

gratuitous distribution as directed by the committee. A copy of the lecture shall be provided by the lecturer for this purpose. The lectures shall be known as "The M. T. Garvin Free Lectures on God and Immortality."

Mr. Garvin named as executors and trustees his bank, Farmers Bank and Trust Company of Lancaster, his physician, Dr. E. T. Prizer, and his lawyer, who is the writer of this introduction. At the time of delivery of the first lecture in 1940, the minister of the Church of Our Father, Unitarian, Lancaster, Pennsylvania, was the Reverend Harvey Swanson; the minister of the First Unitarian Church of Philadelphia, Pennsylvania, was Dr. Frederick R. Griffin; and the minister of the Unitarian Church of Germantown, Pennsylvania, was the Reverend Max F. Daskam. Except for the facts that Dr. Prizer died in 1943, and that Dr. Griffin retired as minister of the First Unitarian Church of Philadelphia in 1947 and has been succeeded by the Reverend Harry B. Scholefield, there has been no change in the personnel of the committee since that time.

The first nine lectures are included in the present volume. In the selection of lecturers, the committee has attempted to carry out the intention of Mr. Garvin and to secure the services of distinguished scholars. The members of the committee hope and believe that the success of this attempt is attested in the pages that follow.

F. LYMAN WINDOLPH

CONTENTS

1

A MODERN CONCEPT OF GOD

Arthur H. Compton

ARTHUR H. COMPTON became chancellor of Washington University, St. Louis, in 1945, having previously served as chairman of the department of physics at the University of Chicago. After many years of X-ray and cosmic-ray research, Dr. Compton became director of the Metallurgical Atomic Project during World War II. Among his numerous awards was the Nobel prize for physics in 1927.

1 *Arthur H. Compton*

A MODERN CONCEPT OF GOD[1]

*J*T IS WITH an intense feeling of my inadequacy that I undertake to present the first Garvin Lecture on the idea of God as affected by modern knowledge. It is clear that I have been selected for this responsibility not because of any unusual familiarity that I might be supposed to have with the traditional religious, theological or philosophical approaches to the subject. Others are far better qualified for such a discussion. I am a man of science, to whom the interpretation of the world comes primarily from the study of nature's laws. I must suppose, therefore, that it is as a man of science that I should discuss this question.

Yet first of all we must ask: Why should we concern ourselves with the idea of God? In foreign lands we find nations willing to fight to be freed from thoughts of God. In our own country multitudes consider the idea of no consequence, and become bored by any discussion of the subject. There are, however, those who feel that life is hardly worth living unless they have confidence in continued fellowship with God. Is he important to us? Any adequate answer to this question must come not from science alone, but from philosophy and religion as well.

Auguste Comte presented long ago what is still considered by many to be the typical position of science. He considered

[1] Delivered at Lancaster, Pennsylvania, as the Garvin Lecture for 1940, under the title, "The Idea of God as Affected by Modern Knowledge."

3

three approaches to knowledge: the primitive or religious approach, based chiefly on superstition, tradition and dogma; the intermediate or philosophical approach, which uses logical analysis as its tool; and the positivistic or scientific approach, a statement of how things are as found by direct observation. He was confident of the ultimate triumph of the latter view of the world. According to him, it is only in unusual phenomena, commonly regarded as miracles, that the idea of God is needed. Ordinary events, following well-known laws, can be interpreted without any such hypothesis. " When science has done its complete work," he predicted, " it will conduct God to the boundary of the universe and bow him out with thanks for his provisional services."

Contrast this with the view held by Isaac Newton, thus paraphrased by Alfred Noyes:

> 'Tis not the lack of links within the chain
> From cause to cause, but that the chain exists;
> That's the unfathomable mystery,
> The one unquestioned miracle that we *know,*
> Implying every attribute of God.[2]

Never was it as clear as it is today that this world has not made itself. How have we ourselves come to be? Is it as a result of our own efforts, or those of our ancestors? In these days of knowledge of the gradual evolution of life, it would be ludicrous to suppose that our coming into being was the result of any dimly formed plan conceived by our invertebrate ancestors. Rather it is clear that forces operating in nature over which we have no control were responsible for the gradual development of life until man appeared on the scene. What are these powers? Scientists try to describe their action by formulating " natural laws." Somehow they are inherent in things, a fundamental part of the universe. For our present purpose we may follow the theologians' nomenclature and call

[2] Alfred Noyes, *Watchers of the Sky* (New York, 1922), pp. 226-227. Copyright, 1922, by J. B. Lippincott and used by their permission.

these higher powers " God." Science, in its efforts to learn the
laws of nature, is in theological language seeking to understand
the way in which God acts. Science is concerned with what
happens, with the actions that occur and with learning the laws
governing these actions. But *action* implies an *actor*, and theology is concerned with the actor. Whether the actor is termed
the universe, nature or God is largely a matter of choice of
words.

In this sense of the actor in all world events, there can be no
question of God's existence. The real problem comes when
we begin to consider his attributes. Is the actor intelligent?
Does he have a plan? Is he interested in the welfare of men and
women? Can he be described as morally good? Such questions
can be answered only by inference from his observed actions,
and in interpreting these actions there is room for difference
of opinion. It is clear, however, that if we mean by God's
actions the events that occur in the world of nature, including
the acts of men as being a part of nature, the study of natural
science is the primary source of the raw material for building
our idea of God.

But the question comes back: Why should we concern ourselves about what God is like? If our study of nature shows
how he acts, is that not enough?

I am convinced that the most fundamental answer to this
question is that which considers the value of life. What are
we here for? Is it the purely biological matter of keeping life
going? Such a view of life's objective is argument in a circle
which gets us nowhere. Is it for our own enjoyment and pleasure? How empty such a life would seem. Or for the pleasure of
our fellows? A better objective, but only more of the same
emptiness. Why then should we live?

Do we not feel that life is most worth while when we know
that we are doing something of lasting value for someone we
love? As we view our evolution from life's primitive beginnings, we can see, though dimly, the outline of a great plan.

Its end we do not see, but we know that we are part of it, and we feel that we can share in promoting it. If this is true, are we not of value to the Planner? I doubt whether there is any objective for life that is ultimately more satisfying than trying to live the life that a man comes to feel his God wants him to live, thus doing his proper part in carrying through the great plan. This is why Jesus placed " Love the Lord thy God with all thy heart " as the first commandment. For, if that love is present, living a life according to his plan will be one's greatest joy.

The writer of the Westminster Catechism expressed the idea simply: " Man's chief end is to glorify God and enjoy him forever."

Such a view of life worth living implies, however, that we can look to our God for understanding and sympathy. We must feel that he knows our weakness as well as our strength. Otherwise there would be no reason for our love and loyalty and a supreme effort to do our part. Some fortunate persons have an immediate awareness of God's presence and comradeship, a religious experience that gives a satisfying basis for love and loyalty. Yet even for these it becomes vital to know whether their intuition is to be classed among superstitions that were better discarded.

It is evident that such attitudes toward God and life are valid only if our knowledge of nature indicates the reasonableness of the view that the Great Actor in world events works according to an intelligent plan, and that he is really concerned with what happens to us. It is this background that accounts for the continued concern with natural theology, the interpretation of God's attributes from the data of science.

I recognize that, in thus presenting the religious basis of my own interest in studying this problem, I expose myself to the charge of wishful thinking in case my conclusions should favor the postulate I have presented for the evaluation of life. I can only reply that if thirty-five years of scientific study have taught me anything it is: first, the danger of letting my preconceptions influence my observations; second, the realization that nothing is as interesting or as valuable as the truth, even though it be contrary to my anticipations; and, third, the habit of practicing the scholarly techniques that avoid the dangers of reaching conclusions predetermined by prejudice. It is a fact that a trained investigator learns by experience that he can rely with surprising confidence upon the conclusions he thus draws when he approaches a problem with an attitude of disinterest.

It is perhaps to be expected that this attitude of scholarly disinterest in the outcome should be confused with indifference with regard to fundamentals of religion. How frequently, because a teacher does not discuss religion in the classroom, merely perhaps because he considers it irrelevant to the subject, it is inferred that he considers religion of negligible value!

The classic example of such false inference is the case of the famous French mathematician Pierre Simon de Laplace. The story is probably authentic that Napoleon, when presented with a copy of Laplace's book on *Celestial Mechanics*, asked: " How is it that you have written this great work on the origin of the world without once mentioning its Creator?" " I don't need that hypothesis," replied Laplace. When this brief story became known, Laplace was identified as an atheist. Yet I can hardly imagine a present-day scholarly presentation of the mechanics of the universe in which introduction of the idea of God would have any place. That the implication of atheism in relation to Laplace was false became evident when, after his death, two of his letters to his son were published in which he urged his son to cultivate companionship with God, since this was the most stable basis for life.

Is God Intelligent?

First among the attributes of God that we must then consider is that of his intelligence. We are to approach this question on the basis of what we see happening in the world. Time permits us to present only a few typical lines of evidence.

If we see in nature evidence of a plan, this will imply intelligence, for a plan or purpose is otherwise meaningless. The alternative to an intelligent plan for the world is that things have happened to be as they are through chance. If we assume infinite time, all possible arrangements of atoms must sometime occur. If then it would appear that the observed arrangement indicates design, we might merely conclude that we happen to live at the time when the world has that form. At another time things would not have shown such an indication.

Here we are concerned with statistics, and the statistical probability of a world's happening to have a form similar to ours is so fantastically small that even in the billions of years that the astronomers might allow for the age of our galaxy it must be considered as highly improbable hypothesis. Alfred Noyes tells how Johannes Kepler discussed this problem:

> Can music rise
> By chance from chaos, as they said that star
> In Serpentarius rose? I told them, then,
> That when I was a boy, with time to spare,
> I played at anagrams. Out of my Latin name
> Johannes Keplerus came that sinister phrase
> Serpens in akuleo. Struck by this,
> I tried again, but trusted it to chance.
> I took some playing-cards, and wrote on each
> One letter of my name. Then I began
> To shuffle them; and, at every shuffle, I read
> The letters, in their order, as they came,
> To see what meaning chance might give to them.
> Wotton, the gods and goddesses must have laughed
> To see the weeks I lost in studying chance;
> For had I scattered those cards into the black
> Epicurean eternity, I'll swear
> They'd still be playing at leap-frog in the dark,
> And show no glimmer of sense. And yet — to hear
> Those wittols talk, you'd think you'd but to mix
> A bushel of good Greek letters in a sack
> And shake them roundly for an age or so,
> To pour the Odyssey out.

> At last, I told
> Those disputants what my wife had said. One night
> When I was tired and all my mind a-dust
> With pondering on their atoms, I was called
> To supper, and she placed before me there
> A most delicious salad. "It would appear,"
> I thought aloud, "that if these pewter dishes,
> Green hearts of lettuce, tarragon, slips of thyme,
> Slices of hard boiled egg, and grains of salt,
> With drops of water, vinegar and oil,
> Had in a bottomless gulf been flying about
> From all eternity, one sure certain day
> The sweet invisible hand of Happy Chance
> Would serve them as a salad."
> "Likely enough,"
> My wife replied. "But not so good as mine,
> Not so well dressed." [2]

Consider the physicist's problem of accounting for the way atoms are formed of a few simple particles, electrons, protons and so on. By various combinations these particles build atoms with remarkable properties. They can group themselves into hundreds of thousands of different molecules, and these in turn into the infinite variety of substances with which we are acquainted, including living organisms with their surprising characteristics. Yet the physicist finds it difficult to select any group of properties for the electrons and protons that will result in anything other than a very dead and dull world. If the simple yet prolific set of pushes and pulls to which the electrons are subject result from pure chance, then chance is more ingenious than the most clever of our scientists.

It is well known, for example, that the carbon atom can form many kinds of molecules. In fact a hundred thousand different carbon compounds would be a conservative estimate. Because of this great chemical versatility, any possible life without carbon would need to be vastly simpler than that which we know.

[2] Noyes, *Watchers of the Sky*, pp. 128-130.

The characteristic feature of the carbon atom is the fact that it contains six electrons. Thus, as Sir Arthur Eddington has remarked, if nature had forgotten the number six, there could be no life as we know it.

Also if atom number six had been as rare as atoms with numbers three, five, nine or ten (lithium, boron, fluorine or neon), life would likewise have been very limited. Or if the properties of the component electrons had been but slightly different, this great versatility, and thus also the chance to produce life, would have been absent. Does carbon just happen to have its distinctive character?

Let us next consider biological evolution. One well-known aspect of this process is that, at each stage of evolution, organisms arise having new characteristics. Thus each of the senses— smell, sight and so on — is a property that could never have been inferred from the properties of more primitive forms such as plants. Life itself, purposive action, and reason, all represent new inventions of nature, whose possibility had previously been hidden. To this phenomenon is given the descriptive name, " emergent evolution."

Equally remarkable is an observation of the paleontologists, who have been primarily responsible for tracing in the rocks the records of life's development. They have shown that changes occur for ages in a single direction, as if a definite experiment were being tried. Instead of variations at random, as Darwin had supposed, this means progress along the same line, generation after generation. A famous example of such " orthogenesis," as it is called, is the evolution of the horse on our Western plains. In natural history museums you can find a row of skeletons arranged in chronological order. It starts with a five-toed horse of the Eocene era, about the size of a dog. As the ages come and go the horses become larger and their toes become fewer until we arrive at the great, single-toed animal that we know today. This is one of the phenomena that lead Professor F. S. C. Northrop of Yale to postulate his

" macroscopic atom," by which he means the universe as an organized intelligent unit, directing its own process toward its chosen objectives.

We should note that the theory of evolution is in no sense an explanation of why these things happen. The scientific doctrine of evolution is concerned wholly with describing how the changes occur — that is, with formulating the laws of biological action. One is reminded of Huxley's comment: " How it is that anything so remarkable as a state of consciousness comes about as a result of irritating nervous tissue is just as unaccountable as the appearance of the Djin when Aladdin rubbed his lamp."

Is it reasonable to suppose that the Powers that made us endowed us with the mystery of consciousness and purposive action, gave us sight and hearing, taught us to enjoy music and the beauties of nature, made it possible for us to understand something of our setting in the world, opened to us the mystery of companionship and love — can it be that these Powers are themselves unconscious of what goes on?

> Was the eye contrived by blindly moving atoms,
> Or the still listening ear fulfilled with music
> By forces without knowledge of sweet sounds?
> Are nerves and brain so sensitively fashioned
> That they convey these pictures of the world
> Into the very substances of our life,
> While that from which we came, the Power that made us,
> Is drowned in blank unconsciousness of it all? [4]

Similar examples could be multiplied indefinitely. Such considerations are those that have led Sir James Jeans in his interpretation of astronomy to conclude that God is the Master Mathematician. The chance that a world such as ours should occur without intelligent design becomes more and more remote as we learn of its wonders.

[4] Noyes, *Watchers of the Sky*, pp. 227-228.

God's Relation to Man

A recent writer has described the conclusion of scientific men from such evidence by the phrase, "God without Religion." He sees the piling up of inescapable evidence of intelligence of the highest order operating in nature, but finds this intelligence so far removed from man that to consider any possible companionship between man and the World Mind would be preposterous. Jeans, in his book, *The Mysterious Universe*, arguing from the exceeding physical insignificance of man in the mighty universe, comes to a somewhat similar conclusion.

Considered from a purely physical point of view this argument may be justified. Man is after all only one of a myriad of organisms that have infected the crust of a minor planet of one of the smaller stars in one of a billion galaxies. Even on the crust of his planet his handiwork has had vastly less effect than the vegetation that has completely altered the composition of the atmosphere, put carbon into the ground and covered with a green coat most of the dry land. What matter if man should be destroyed? It would merely be the closing act of a minor side show in the great celestial circus.

But why should we suppose that physical size or power should be the basis for the value estimates of an intelligent God? When a ship sinks at sea, where is our great concern? Is it not with its precious cargo of men rather than with the great hulk of steel and powerful engines? Ask a mother which is more important, the brightest star in the heavens or her newborn babe. Even to an astronomer, if the child should be a Newton, his value would be greater than that of a whole galaxy of stars.

For value depends upon the interests of the judge. Might we not reasonably assume that an intelligent Creator would find his intelligent creatures of especial interest? The great effort through which nature has gone to bring life to its present condition would certainly seem to point in that direction.

We may then properly inquire: Where in this universe is intelligent life to be found? We know life on earth. As we observe it, organic life requires molecules of a complex type which occur only under limited conditions of temperature and an abundance of the necessary chemical elements. Basing our judgment on our experience that intelligence seems confined to highly developed organisms, we will not expect to find intelligent life on the stars, where the excessively high temperatures rule out any except the simplest molecules. As we look to the planets in our own solar system, we find the moon bare of life, and the major planets — Jupiter, Saturn and so on — too cold to support life. Venus and Mercury seem too hot, and the carbon-dioxide atmosphere of Venus seems to show the absence of vegetation there. On Mars, on the other hand, the red oxide of iron which gives the planet its ruddy color can hardly have been formed without abundant oxygen in the atmosphere, which must have been put there by growing vegetation. Thus, of the places we can study, the earth and Mars are the only two that have appropriate conditions for the development of life, and both seem to be the abode of life.

With the immense number of stars in the heavens, it might naturally be supposed that there are myriad other planetary systems like that of our sun on which life may likewise have developed. Perhaps so. But if present theories of the origin of our solar system are correct — explaining planets by the close approach of two stars — the extreme rarity of such an encounter would make planets correspondingly rare. Such considerations have led Sir Arthur Eddington, after most careful and competent study of this problem, to conclude:

I do not think that the whole purpose of creation has been staked on the one planet where we live; and in the long run we cannot deem ourselves the only race that has been or will be gifted with the mystery of consciousness. But I feel inclined to claim that at the present time our race is supreme; and not one of the profusion of stars in their myriad clusters looks down on scenes comparable to those which are passing beneath the rays of the sun.[5]

Not all astronomers agree with this conclusion. Some consider planetary systems to be much more common. I have myself been sufficiently convinced by the arguments that Eddington presents to base my own thinking on the assumption that life throughout the universe is very rare.

One might consider this as direct evidence that the Creator of the universe is not concerned with life. We might equally well conclude that, because only one maple seed in a million grows to the maturity of a great forest tree, the growth of trees is no concern of the maker of the seeds. The evidence of the earth and Mars gives good reason to believe that the world is so constituted that, wherever a planet exists under the proper conditions, life will appear. Considering the most remarkable properties, both physical and intellectual, that life exhibits, can it be that our Creator has just chanced upon this accident of his creation?

Out in Sequoia National Park is a group of giant redwood trees, one of which is supposed to be the oldest living thing, towering high above all other trees of the forest. Each tree is a monument that could be replaced only by the ages. Fortunately our government is giving them careful protection. If by some disaster one is destroyed, nature has others that may develop to their full majesty. But the number of trees is limited, and, to those who love trees, it is of vital interest to see that each healthy one is given a full opportunity for growth.

Is not the life of man on earth similar to that of one of these great trees? No doubt there are or will be other places where similar or perhaps higher types of life than ours may be developed. But there is reason to believe that we occupy a relatively high position in the universe with respect to intelligent

[5] Arthur Eddington, *Nature of the Physical World* (Cambridge, England, 1928), p. 178. Copyright, 1928, by The Macmillan Company and used by their permission.

life. Does it seem then too bold to assume that the Creator — whose intelligence has seemed to us much the most reasonable explanation of our world — should take an especial interest in the welfare of the perhaps uniquely intelligent beings that he has created?

Let us ask ourselves then whether the evidence indicates that God is friendly toward man. Forget for the moment any evidence of an intelligence working in the world, and consider it as a vast machine. Our study of science emphasizes the fact that the laws by which this machine operates are immutable; nevertheless, when we begin to understand them we can turn them to our service. As was perhaps first seen clearly by Pythagoras, if we learn these laws and live in accord with nature's rules, we and our fellows have a fuller and a happier life.

From the observed uniformity and universal applicability of nature's laws, it would be quite unreasonable to suppose that the world plays favorites by showing partiality toward man. Rather we find that the laws of nature are such that under conditions existing on earth a group of living organisms, of which man stands foremost in intellectual development, evolve as a matter of course. As a part of this evolution, his physical adaptability and reasoning powers have undoubtedly arisen through the strict working of natural laws. According to this law it is clear that hardships have had to be surmounted. In the agelong struggle with other animals, cunning and craft have developed. To gain needed shelter and food, inventiveness has been at a premium. In order to live in satisfactory relations with other men, a conscience has evolved.

At each stage of this development there has been tragic, apparently ruthless, suffering. This has been nature's method of forcing slowly developing humanity to search for and follow the better way. It would be hard to imagine a process for achieving adaptation to environment that would be more certainly effective than the one we see now working in nature. With regard to our distinctively human characteristics we are, however, clearly in the early stages of evolution. A short thousand generations ago man was a lone hunter, like the tiger. Gradually he is becoming a social animal, more nearly similar to the ant, with special functions and skills. With the growth of his scientific and technical knowledge, his community grows to a larger and larger scale, until it approaches a planetary organization. Along with this social evolution arise new responsibilities, new types of mutual adjustment, the need for new codes of morals. It is evident that, with regard to such attributes as the understanding of the world, the use of the powers of nature, the perfection of social organization, and the consideration of one's fellows, our remote descendants may be expected to reach much higher levels than ours.

In any case, the result of the evolutionary process has been that, when we learn nature's laws and school ourselves to obey them, we can turn them to our advantage. That is, these laws are friendly to well-adapted organisms. But, because only the satisfactorily adapted organisms survive in the struggle for life, it is those that are well adjusted to their surroundings that always form the predominant group. It is for this reason that, without any kind of partiality, the laws of nature bring into being only those creatures to which nature's laws are on the whole friendly.

Is nature then friendly to us? Assuredly, if we will learn her laws and discipline ourselves to live accordingly. If we do not, she simply eliminates our kind from her world.

Is the God thus revealed by nature severe? Certainly no more so than the God of the Bible. " All things work together for good for him who serves the Lord " is the exact parallel of nature's laws that are friendly to the well-adapted organism. On the other hand, nature's uncompromising attitude toward the man who will not so adapt himself is accurately caught in Paul's proverb, " The wages of sin is death." Jesus himself pictures the Father as adamant in removing from among his children those who will not accept his principles of love as the guide for love:

If a man abide not in me, he is cast forth as a branch and is withered; and they gather them and cast them into the fire, and they are burned. . . . If ye keep my commandments, ye shall abide in my love.[6]

Is this less severe than the evolutionists' nature which eliminates the individuals and species unfit for survival?

Is God Good?

There are certain theological difficulties raised by the view of the relationship between God and man that has just been developed. These I am in no position to discuss with authority. They should, however, be mentioned so that following Garvin lecturers with more adequate theological background may see them as viewed in the light of scientific approach.

The first is God's undoubted responsibility for permitting evil to be present in the world, if our view is correct that the laws of nature represent his mode of action. There seems no avoidance of the conclusion that, if we ascribe to God the beauties of the world, we must likewise hold him responsible for the most ugly crimes. This point has been forcibly presented by Bishop Barnes, with the conclusion:

For some unknown reason He permitted death, disease, struggle, the instincts which have led to selfishness and lust in man, because He willed that higher moral, intellectual and emotional development which in man is such an unexpected outcome of the process.[7]

It would indeed seem that from the very nature of the evolutionary method such evils must be present in order that man's moral character shall develop. But what shall we say regarding God's character? Is he nonmoral? Perhaps some future Garvin lecturer will describe how the effort to reconcile this

---

[6] John 15: 6, 10.

[7] E. W. Barnes, *Scientific Theory and Religion* (Cambridge, England, 1933), pp. 520-522. Used by permission of The Macmillan Company.

evil in God's world with the idea of his goodness leads to one of the classical arguments for immortality.

The second problem is that of God's mercy toward men, so confidently taught by Jesus. There appears but little mercy in the severe discipline by which the mills of the gods grind out organisms adapted to their environment. The description of nature as " red in tooth and claw " describes only too well man's relations with man as well as the life of animals. Where then is God's mercy?

My impression is that this mercy is very real, but is to be found in the psychological rather than the physical realm. The knowledge that one has done his best, though in vain, the recognition that both God and our fellows know the limitations and frailties of our human nature and do not expect of us more than our strength permits, these protect us from the too keen cutting edge of conscience. Here it is that a sane, well-balanced religion, which helps men to feel the understanding and sympathetic presence of their Creator, offers the solace for which all yearn.

Men Become God's Children

We find then that through a period of a billion years life has gradually developed on this planet. Throughout vast ages all responsibility for that growth lay with the God of nature. At least on our planet no conscious living being was in a position to do more than what he was made to do. The world was, so to speak, a great mechanical toy — complex, it is true, but functioning only according to the dictates of its controlling laws. During this period primitive men at last appeared on the scene. They were like their animal cousins, caring only for themselves. The findings of students of prehistoric man show all too clearly that he considered his fellows as other animals, as beasts of burden or as food. At last man tasted of the fruit of the tree of knowledge, and began to distinguish good from evil. Before that time, in spite of his cleverness, man's actions in helping or destroying his fellows were done in the same spirit of innocence in which wolf helps wolf in the attack on an enemy, or turns to eat his wounded mate. Now a new kind of being emerged. He found that his acts had lasting effects for good or for ill upon his own life and that of his fellows, and he *cared* about the result. Here was the dawn of conscience.

Now there was a being that consciously tried to make his world better. He was able to adapt his environment to fit his needs. As his knowledge of tools and weapons increased, he became master of the plant and animal life on earth, and tamed them to serve him. Gradually he has come to control, to a large extent, even his own life and future. A share of the responsibility for the development of the earth as a place to live was now shifted to man's shoulders.

According to my late colleague, Dr. James Breasted, who spent a lifetime studying the social growth of man, this dawn of conscience came to man surprisingly recently, only some five or six thousand years ago. We might well ask whether man has yet learned that he is his brother's keeper. But now, with our growing understanding and power of science, the transfer of authority is gradually being extended. Considering the obvious errors that we are making we may be thankful that we do not yet have complete control of our development. Yet now we can feel that we are sharing with our Creator the great task that he has undertaken. As junior partners, taking our part of the responsibility, or as his children, taken at last into the household, we can truly say, " My Father worketh hitherto, and I work."

Science can have no quarrel with a religion that postulates a God to whom men are as his children. It is possible to see the whole great drama of evolution as leading toward the goal of the making of persons, with free, intelligent wills, capable of learning nature's laws, of seeing dimly God's purpose in nature, and of working with him to make that purpose effective.

Science has thus helped us to appreciate the inspiring setting in which we find ourselves. We recognize the greatness of the program of nature which is unfolding before us, and we feel that we are an essential part of a great enterprise in which a mighty Intelligence is working out his hidden plan. In our hands we hold the conditions of life on this planet. If indeed the creation of intelligent persons is a major objective of the Creator of the Universe, and if, as we have reason to surmise, mankind is his highest development in this direction, the opportunity and responsibility of working as God's partners in his great task should inspire us to the highest achievement of which we are capable. What nobler ambition can a man have than to co-operate with his Maker in bringing about a better world in which to live?

> Ye prate of patterns and the web of doom.
> Is God then strangled in the warp and woof?
> Is not the Weaver in the Weaver's place?
> Go seat you at the loom!
> Create the goodness that is heaven's proof,
> And work with God, if ye would see his face! [8]

[8] E. H. Lewis, "Mater Humanissima" in *University of Chicago Poems* (Chicago, 1923). Used by permission of the University of Chicago Press.

2

THE IMMORTALITY OF MAN

Jacques Maritain

JACQUES MARITAIN, recently appointed professor of philosophy by Princeton University, was the postwar French ambassador to the Vatican. Converted to Catholicism in 1906, he began the study of scholastic philosophy two years later. Many of his books have been translated into English, including *Art and Scholasticism, Freedom in the Modern World, The Rights of Man and Natural Law, Existence and the Existent* and *Art and Poetry*.

2 *Jacques Maritain*

THE IMMORTALITY OF MAN [1]

I

*L*ET US THINK of the human being, not in an abstract and general way, but in the most concrete possible, the most *personal* fashion. Let us think of a certain old man we have known for years in the country — this old farmer with his wrinkled face, his keen eyes which have beheld so many harvests and so many earthly horizons, his long habits of patience and suffering, courage, poverty and noble labor. Or let us think of certain boys or girls who are our relatives or our friends, whose everyday life we well know, and whose loved appearance, whose soft or husky voice, is enough to rejoice our hearts. Let us remember — remember in our heart — a single gesture of the hand, or the smile in the eyes of one we love. What treasures on earth, what masterpieces of art or of science, could pay for the treasures of life, feeling, freedom and memory, of which this gesture, this smile, is the fugitive expression? We perceive intuitively that nothing in the world is more precious than one single human being. I am well aware how many difficult questions come to mind at the same time and I shall come back to these difficulties, but for the present I wish only to keep in mind this simple and decisive intuition, by means of which the incomparable value of the human person is revealed to us. Moreover, St. Thomas Aquinas warns us that the Person is what is noblest and most perfect in the whole of nature.

[1] Delivered at Lancaster, Pennsylvania, as the Garvin Lecture for 1941.

23

Nothing, however, nothing in the world is more squandered, more wasted, than a human being. Nothing is spent so prodigally, so heedlessly, as though a man were a bit of small change in the hand of careless Nature. Surely it is a crime to throw away human lives more cruelly and contemptuously than the lives of cattle, to submit them to the merciless will-to-power of totalitarian states or of insatiate conquerors. The present-day transportations of populations, concentration camps, wars of enslavement, are signs of a criminal contempt for mankind unheard of until now. Surely it is shameful as well to contemplate throughout the world the debasing standards of life imposed on so many human beings in their slums of distress and starvation. As Burke wrote a century and a half ago, " The blood of man should never be shed but to redeem the blood of man. It is well shed for our family, for our friends, for our God, for our country, for our kind. The rest is vanity; the rest is crime." Yet since the blood of man is well shed for our family, for our friends, for our country, for our kind, for our God, this very fact shows that many things are indeed worth a man's sacrifice of his earthly life. What things? Things of a truly human and divine value, things that involve and preserve that justice, that freedom, that sacred respect for truth and for the dignity of the spirit without which human existence becomes unlivable; things that a man may and should love more than his own flesh and blood, just because they pertain to the great task of redeeming the blood of man.

But what I should like to emphasize is the fact that in the obscure workings of the human species, in that immense network of solidarity each mesh of which is made of human effort and human risk and advances in its small way the progression of the whole, there is an infinity of things, often of little things, for which men expose themselves to danger and self-sacrifice. Often the reasons for such lavish courage are not love or pure generosity, but only natural energy, or temerity, or longing for glory, or pleasure in confronting new difficulties, or desire for risk and adventure. All these, however, are carried away in that flood of superabundance and self-giving which springs from the sources of being, and which brings mankind toward its fulfillment. A scientist risks his life for a new discovery in the realm of matter, a pioneer to establish a new settlement, an aviator to improve our means of communication, a miner to extract coal from the earth, a pearl fisher to filch from the ocean an ornament for the beauty of some unknown woman, a traveler to contemplate new landscapes, a mountain climber to conquer a bit of earth. What comparison is there between the result to be obtained, be it momentous or slight, and the price of human life which is thus wagered, the value of that being, full of promise, endowed with so many gifts and whom many hearts may love? Well, at each corner of human activity death lies in ambush. Every day we trust our lives and those of our beloved to the unknown driver of a subway train, of a plane, of a bus or a taxi. Where there is no risk, there is no life. A wisdom or a civilization based on the avoidance of risk, by virtue of a misinterpretation of the value of the human being, would run the greatest of all risks, that of cowardice and of deadly stupidity. That perpetual risk which man takes is the very condition of his life. That squandering of the human being is a law of nature; it is also the proof of the confidence, the trust and the elementary love we give every day to the divine principle from which we proceed, the very law of which is superabundance and generosity.

Now we face a paradox: on the one hand nothing in the world is more precious than one single human person; on the other hand nothing in the world is more squandered, more exposed to all kinds of dangers than the human being — and this condition must be. What is the meaning of this paradox? It is perfectly clear. We have here a sign that man knows very well that death is not an end, but a beginning. He knows very well, in the secret depths of his own being, that he can run all risks, spend his life and scatter his possessions here below, because he is immortal. The chant of the Christian liturgy before the body of the deceased is significant: Life is changed, life is not taken away.

II

As I have just noted, there is in man a natural, an instinctive knowledge of his immortality. This knowledge is inscribed not in man's intelligence, but rather in his ontological structure; it is rooted not in the principles of reasoning, but in his very substance. The intelligence may become aware of this knowledge in an indirect way, through some reflection, some turning back of thought upon the recesses of human subjectivity. The intelligence may also ignore this instinctive knowledge, and remain unaware of it, for our intelligence is naturally turned or diverted toward the being of external things. It may even deny the soul and immortality, by virtue of any set whatsoever of ideas and reasonings; yet, when the intellect of a man denies immortality, this man continues living, despite his rational convictions, on the basis of an unconscious and, so to speak, biological assumption of this very immortality — though it is rationally denied. Although such discrepancies are not infrequent among us, introducing many troubles, deviations or weaknesses into our behavior, they cannot disturb or annihilate the basic prerequisites of that behavior.

The instinctive knowledge of which I speak is a common and obscure knowledge. When a man is not an " intellectual " man — that is to say, when his intelligence, rarely busy with ideas, science and philosophy, follows for guidance only the natural tendencies of our species — this instinctive knowledge naturally reverberates in his mind. He does not doubt that another life will come after the present one. The possibility of doubt and error about what is most natural in the basic strata of human existence is the price paid for the progress of our species toward its rational fulfillment. Sometimes it is a very high price! The only solution, however, is not to try some sort of return to purely instinctive life, as D. H. Lawrence and many others have dreamed it. This regression, moreover, is quite impossible, and could only lead, not to nature, but to a perversion of civilized life. The only solution worthy of man is not a backward flight toward instinct, but a flight ahead toward reason, toward a reason that at last is well equipped and knows the truth.

Of man's instinctive belief in his immortality, which is not a conceptual or philosophical knowledge, but a lived and practiced one, we have a striking sign in the behavior of primitive men. No matter how far back we look into the past, we always find the trace of funeral rites, of an extraordinary care about the dead and their life beyond the grave. What we know concerning the beliefs of primitive men shows us that their belief in immortality might assume the strangest and most aberrant forms. Sometimes, as in the old Chinese superstitions, the dead were terribly feared, and the living man was to take every precaution against their mischievousness. In any case, the ideas, the reasons and explanations by means of which primitive men sought to justify their belief and to imagine the survival of the dead seem to us very queer, often absurd. This oddness and absurdity of primitive mythologies, which Frazer emphasized with the naïveté of the civilized man, are easily explainable. On the one hand the mental climate of the primitive man is not the climate of reason, but that of imagination; the intelligence of primitive men — a very acute and awakened one, vitally immersed in nature — functions in a kind of dusk where the imagination rules. Their conceptions are regulated by the law of images. When this point is well understood, the myths of primitive men appear less absurd, much wiser even than some anthropologists believe. On the other hand, as regards belief in immortality, the conceptions of primitive man are not the result of any rational inquiry. On the contrary they only translate, according to the ebb and flow of the imaginative thought, a substantial — not intellectual — persuasion given him by nature. The more irrational and queer his myths of the soul and its survival appear, the more strikingly they give testimony to the fact that his certitude of survival is rooted in underground strata more profound and immovable, though less perfect and fertile, than the arable soil of reason.

How then can we explain the origin of the natural and instinctive knowledge of immortality? Here we must consider that the highest functions of the human mind, particularly the functions of judgment, are performed in the midst of a kind of consciousness that is vital and spontaneous and accompanies every achieved or perfected act of thought. This spontaneous or *concomitant* consciousness is to be carefully distinguished from the consecutive or *explicit* consciousness. The second one presupposes a special reflexive act, by means of which the mind comes back upon itself and produces special reflexive concepts, special reflexive judgments concerning what lies within itself. The concomitant consciousness does not do so. It only expresses the self-interiority, the self-involvement proper to the human mind; it is only the diffuse light of reflexivity — lived and practiced, not conceptualized — within which every spiritual achievement is accomplished in the human soul. But such a spontaneous consciousness slips back to the very root and principle of our mental operations, attains this root as something unknown in itself, known only — and that is enough, moreover — as transcending all operations and psychic phenomena that proceed from it. The Self, the supraphenomenal Self, is thus obscurely but certainly attained by the spontaneous consciousness — in the night as regards every notion and conceptualization, with certainty as regards vital experience. This experience — not conceptually formulated, but practically lived by the intellect — of a supraphenomenal Self is the basic datum, the rock of spontaneous consciousness. Our intelligence knows that, before thinking of it; this obscure knowledge is involved in every achieved act of thought, dealing with any matter whatsoever. When philosophical reflection forms and elaborates the idea of the Self, it attains thereby an object that human intelligence already knew — in a merely lived and unexpressed fashion — and now recognizes.

Human intelligence also knows — in the same obscure fashion — that this supraphenomenal Self, vitally grasped by spontaneous consciousness, cannot disappear — precisely because it is grasped as a center that dominates all passing phenomena, the whole succession of temporal images. That is to say, the Self, the knower able to know its own existence, is superior to time. All perceptions and images that succeed one another, composing the fluent show of this world, may vanish, as happens when a man sleeps without dreaming. The Self cannot vanish, because death, as well as sleep, is an event in time, and the Self is above time. This vivid perception — even if it remains unformulated, in the state of some intellectual feeling rather than of any conceptualized statement — is, I believe, the very origin of that instinctive knowledge of man's immortality which we are now considering.

Another point must be added, concerning the aspirations proper to the Self rather than the spontaneous consciousness of it. When philosophers look upon this metaphysical reality which is called Personality, they establish that a Person is essentially a spiritual totality, characterized by independence. A Person is a universe to itself, a universe of knowledge, love and freedom, a whole which cannot be subordinated as a part, except with regard to such wholes to which it can be related through the instrumentality of knowledge and of love. Personality is an analogical and transcendental perfection, which is fully realized only in God, the Pure Act. Then philosophers are led to distinguish in the human Person two different types of aspirations. Certain aspirations of the Person are *connatural* to man. These concern the human Person insofar as it possesses a determinate specific nature. Other aspirations may be called *transnatural*. And these concern the human Person precisely in so far as it is a person and participates in the transcendental perfection of personality. Now, among the aspirations of the Person, the most obvious one is the aspiration toward not-dying. Death, the destruction of Self, is for the human Self not so much a thing to be feared as it is first of all a thing incomprehensible, impossible, an offense, a scandal. Not to be is nonsense for the person. This is so true that, although we meet death at every step, although we see our relatives, our friends die, although we attend their burial, still the most difficult thing for us is to believe in the reality of death. Man sees death; he does not believe in it. Yet the human Person does not escape dying, so that it may seem that his aspiration toward immortality is thus deceived. How is this possible? We know very well that an aspiration that expresses only the very structure of a being cannot be deceived. The only way is to distinguish, according to the distinction I indicated a moment ago, what is connatural and what is transnatural in the aspiration with which we are dealing.

To the extent that it relates to the spiritual part of the human whole, to the soul, the aspiration toward not-dying is connatural to man, and cannot be deceived. To the extent that it relates to the whole itself, to the human Person made up of soul and body, this aspiration is a transnatural aspiration. It can be deceived. Yet, even when deceived, it remains within us, appealing to we know not what power, appealing to the very principle of being for we know not what kind of realization beyond death — beyond the corruption of that body which is an essential part of the human whole and without which the individual soul is not, truly speaking, a Person — beyond every evidence of the disappearance of the Person scattered amidst the glamorous appearances of Nature and the seasons — beyond this very world the existence and duration of which is linked with the generation and corruption of material substances and is therefore a denial of the human Person's very claim to immortality.

III

I have spoken of the instinctive and natural, lived and practiced, belief in man's immortality. Now I should like to pass to philosophical knowledge, to that kind of knowledge, no longer instinctive and natural, but rational and elaborated, by means of which the human mind can achieve perfectly tested or demonstrated certitudes.

The philosophical knowledge of which I speak is not positivism, because positivism seems to be a despair of philosophy rather than a philosophy; however, the father of all modern positivists, Auguste Comte, felt so strongly the inescapability of the problem of immortality that he tried to answer it according to his possibilities, and granted a major part, in his positivist religion of Humanity, to what he called the *subjective* immortality, the immortality of everyone, in the memory, thought and love of those who knew him and appreciated him. Naturally, as regards Auguste Comte himself, the immortality he would thus enjoy was to be the eternal gratitude of all mankind. I am very far from despising this subjective immortality. To be preserved within a mind, to endure in minds as something known and told in song and story, is an enviable condition for material things, and precisely the kind of immortality they will enjoy. Events in human history groan after their epic and wait for their poet; this world will be immortal in the memories of immortal spirits, and in the stories they will tell one another about it. But if subjective immortality is something, it is precisely because there are immaterial minds which may receive in themselves the images of what is perishable. Subjective immortality would be nothing — or a derision — if objective immortality, genuine immortality, did not exist.

The philosophical reasons that testify to immortality may be expounded in the following way. First, human intelligence is able to know whatever participates in being and truth; the whole universe can be inscribed in it; that is to say, the object it knows has been previously deprived, in order to be known, of any conditions of materiality: What is the weight and volume of my idea of man? Does man possess any dimension or perform any transmutation of energy within my mind? Does the sun exert any heating action within my intellect? Nay more, intellectual knowledge is abstract and universal knowledge. This rose (which I am seeing) has contours; but being (which I am thinking of) is vaster than space. The object of intelligence is something universal, which remains what it is while being identified to an infinity of individuals. And that is possible only because things, in order to become objects of the intellect, have been entirely separated from their material existence by the intellect itself. The objects known by human intelligence, taken not as things existing in themselves, but precisely as objects determining intelligence and united with it, are immaterial.

The second point: Just as is the condition of the object, so is the condition of the act that bears on it and is determined or specified by it. The object of human intelligence is as such immaterial; the act of the human intelligence is also immaterial.

The third point: Since the act of the intellectual power is immaterial, this power itself is also immaterial. Intelligence is in man an immaterial power. Doubtless it depends on the body, on the conditions of the brain. Its activity can be disturbed or hindered by physical trouble, by an outburst of anger, by a drink, by a narcotic. But this dependence is an *extrinsic* one. It exists because our intelligence cannot act without the joint activity of memory and imagination, of internal senses and external senses, all of which are organic powers, residing in some material organ, in some special part of the body. As to intelligence itself, it is not *intrinsically* dependent on the body, since its activity is immaterial; human intelligence does not reside in any special part of the body. It uses the brain, since the organs of the internal senses are in the brain; yet the brain is not the organ of the intelligence: there is no part of the organism whose act is intellectual operation. The intellect has no organ.

And the final point: Since intellectual power is immaterial, its first substantial root, the very substance from which it emanates and which acts through its instrumentality, is also immaterial. An immaterial soul must be the first substantial root of an immaterial psychic soul-power. It is conceivable that such an immaterial soul have, besides immaterial faculties, other powers and activities that are organic and material. For this immaterial soul is not only a spirit, but also a spirit made for animating a body, in Aristotelian terms a " substantial form," an *entelechy* which by its union with matter constitutes a particular corporeal substance, the human being. But it would be perfectly inconceivable that a material soul, a soul that informs a body — as the souls of animals and plants do, according to the biological philosophy of Aristotle — but that is not a spirit and cannot exist without informing matter, should possess a power or faculty (that is, should act through an instrumentality) that is immaterial, intrinsically independent of any corporeal organ and physical structure.

Thus the human soul is both a soul — that is, the first principle of life in a living body — and a spirit, able to exist and to live apart from matter. The human soul has its own immaterial existence and its own immaterial subsistence: and it is by virtue of this immaterial existence and subsistence of the human soul that each element of the human body is human and exists as such. The radical immateriality of the highest operations of the human soul, of intellectual knowledge, of contemplation, of suprasensuous love and desire and joy, of free will, is an evidence that this soul is spiritual in itself, and cannot cease existing and living. It cannot be corrupted, since it has no matter; it cannot be disintegrated, since it has no substantial parts; it cannot lose its individual unity, since it is self-subsisting, or its internal energy, since it contains within itself all the sources of its energies. The human soul cannot die. Once existing, it cannot disappear; it will necessarily exist always, endure without end.

Each one of us is inhabited. With what wonderful respect we would look upon every human being, if we thought of that invisible Psyche who dwells within him and who causes him to be what he is, and who will endure longer than the world, endure always, after these poor bones are reduced to dust! How can our eyes contemplate any human person without seeking anxiously after the eternal mystery which is living in him? The first Christians kissed the breasts of their children with awe and veneration, thinking of that eternal presence within them. They had some idea, some awareness, less fickle than ours, of the immortality of the human soul.

I have just considered the immortality of the human soul. All the certitudes which the wisdom of philosophers brings forth concerning immortality deal with the immortality of the human *soul*, because non-cessation of being is the natural property of what is spiritual in us. But what of those aspirations of the human Person toward immortality that I emphasized a moment ago? These aspirations concern the very Person, Man himself, the natural whole made of flesh and spirit — not the human soul alone. About the aspiration of man to the immortality of *man*, not merely of the *human soul*, the philosophical reason has very little to say.

On the one hand, philosophical reason perceives that a separate soul is not a person, although it subsists in itself. It is not a person, because the notion of Person is essentially the notion of a complete and perfect whole. The body integrates the natural human totality, and the soul is only a part. What would be the life of separated souls, if they had to lead a merely natural life? They would live a truly pale life in a pallid paradise, like the Elysian fields of the ancients, with their pallid asphodels. Separated souls in a merely natural condition would not see God face to face — a supernatural privilege; they would know

God through that image of God which is themselves, and they would know themselves in an intuitive manner. They would be dazzled by their own beauty, the beauty of a spiritual substance, and they would know other things in a confused and imperfect way, through the instrumentality of their substance, in the measure in which the other things resemble them. But all this knowledge would remain in a kind of dusk, because of the natural weakness of human intellect. Moreover all the sensible powers of the human soul, sensible memory, imagination, instinct and passion, as well as external senses, remain asleep in a separated soul — in such a way that if there were not a supernatural compensation and supercompensation for such a soul, the happy life it would live, according to its natural condition, would be a half life in happiness.

On the other hand, philosophical reason understands that, since the human soul is naturally made to animate a body, a kind of unfulfillment, incompleteness and substantial dissatisfaction must remain in the separated soul, in regard to that other half of the human being which the soul, by virtue of its very being, tends to use for its own purpose and operations, while giving it ontological consistence and activity. And in this way philosophical reason wonders whether such a desire for reunion with the body could not some day be fulfilled in the immortal soul. Yes, as regards God's omnipotence, there is no impossibility of some re-embodiment of the soul in its flesh and bones, and some restoration of the human integrity. But human reason can only conceive this possibility; it cannot go farther, and therefore, as concerns the supreme aspiration of the human Person toward immortality, toward the immortality of Man, human reason stops, remains silent and dreams.

IV

This question, however, must be asked: In point of fact, will this aspiration toward the immortality of the human Person remain forever unsatisfied? Such a question transcends the philosophical domain, the domain of human reason. The problem is a religious one; it engages and puts into play the deepest, the most crucial religious conceptions of mankind.

Two great conceptions here confront each other. They represent the two types of religious interpretation of human life which are alone possible. One conception is the Indian conception, the other is the Judaeo-Christian one.

The Indian conception surrenders the immortality of the person, and teaches metempsychosis or transmigration. The soul is immortal, but the soul transmigrates. At the death of the body, the soul passes to another body, like a bird to a new cage, a more or less noble, more or less painful new cage, according to the merits or demerits gathered by the soul during its previous life. Thus there is for the same soul a succession of personalities as well as a succession of lives; each of these personalities slips away forever, will never appear again, like outworn coats that a man throws away from season to season. The unlimited flux, the irremediable disappearance of the successive personalities, is the ransom for the immortality of the soul.

There are very impressive and definite philosophical arguments against the idea of transmigration. The essential argument is the following: transmigration implies that each soul preserves its own individuality and yet passes from one body to another. But that is possible only if the soul is not substantially one with the body. The negation of the substantial unity of man, and the negation of the fact that soul and personality are inseparably joined — such a soul, such a personality; such a personality, such a soul — these two negations are inevitably involved in the doctrine of transmigration. That is to say, there is transmigration if man is not man; or, as Aristotle said, if the art of the flute-player can descend into the harp and cause the harp to produce the sound of the flute. The basic truth concerning the human being, the substantial unity of man, is incompatible with the idea of transmigration.

But despite the strength of this philosophical evidence, the idea of transmigration remains a temptation for the religious consciousness of mankind. Why this temptation toward metempsychosis? In my opinion this temptation results from the conflict between the idea of the sanction for human acts and the idea of the brevity, distress and foolishness of human life. How is it possible that a man's unhappy life, with all its insignificance, blundering and wretchedness, should open suddenly out upon Eternity? How is it possible that an eternal reward or retribution, an eternal and immutable end, may be fixed for us in virtue of some good or bad movements of so weak and queer, so dormant a free will as ours? The disproportion is too great between the End and the Means. I imagine that the mind of India was discouraged and frightened by such an idea, and therefore fell back, so to speak, into the infinity of time, as if a series of new lives offered to the same soul would somehow avail to attenuate the disproportion I just emphasized between the precariousness of the journey and the importance of its end.

Yes, but then there is no longer an end. Time continues always to be Time. The mind finds itself confronted with the horror of an endless series of reincarnations. The very law of transmigration becomes a terrible and intolerable law, of new suffering ceaselessly assumed, new trials, new pain amidst new vanishing and torturing appearances. The idea of Nirvana will then occur as a way of escape. But Nirvana is only a deliverance from Time. As it is conceived by Indian metaphysics (I do not say as it is lived in fact by such or such contemplative soul), Nirvana is only an escape, the self-annihilation of that very transmigration that was to bring about the immortality of the soul, and that now abolishes itself, and along with itself immortality. Transmigration was not a solution — it was an escape, a flight, from which in turn escape must be sought.

The Judaeo-Christian conception is a philosophy of the final end, and the philosophy of the final end is the exact contrary of the philosophy of transmigration. The pursuit of immortality through a horizontal movement all along a time without end is quite different from, is the exact opposite of, the vertical fulfillment of immortality by the attainment of an End that is eternal and infinite — just as Nirvana is quite different from, and in a sense the exact opposite of, the passage to eternity and the possession of everlasting life. What makes the Judaeo-Christian solution possible is in part a true appreciation of the relationship between time and eternity: lengthen time as much as you will, add years to years, hoard up lives upon lives, but time will ever remain having no common measure with eternity; a thousand transmigrations are as little before eternity as is the short life of this particular poor little child; this short human life is as much before eternity as a thousand transmigrations. But what makes the Judaeo-Christian solution possible is also and above all the fact that in it the philosophy of the last End is involved in the whole of the truths and mysteries of divine revelation. Let us understand that God is personal, Life and Truth and Love in Person; let us understand that there is a supernatural order, and that the least degree of grace — that is, of participation in the inner life of God himself — is more valuable than all the splendor of this star-strewn universe; let us understand that God has taken flesh in the womb of a virgin of Israel in order to die for mankind and to infuse in us the life of his own blood; let us understand that the free initiatives and resources, the patience and the ingenuity of the mercy of God are exceedingly greater than the weakness or the wickedness of our human free will. Then we understand that that disproportion between the precariousness of the journey and the importance of the end, which I emphasized above, is in reality counterbalanced, and even exceedingly compensated for, by the generosity and the *humanity*, as St. Paul put it, of our Savior God. Man does not save himself through his own power: it is God and Christ who save man through the power of the Cross and of divine grace, by the instrumentality of Faith and Charity fructifying in good works.

The Judaeo-Christian conception is not only a philosophy of the last End but also, and by the same stroke, a philosophy of the immortality of Man. It asserts not only the immortality of the Soul, but also the immortality of the human Person, of the whole human subject — because grace perfects Nature and fulfills supereminently the aspirations of Nature, those aspirations of the human person which I have already called *transnatural*. What the sacred writings of the Jews constantly emphasized, what mattered most to them, was not so much the immortality of the soul as the resurrection of the body. It is the resurrection of the body that St. Paul preached in Athens, to the astonishment of the philosophers. It is the resurrection of the body that we Christians hope for: a resurrection which transcends all the powers of nature, and which is to be accomplished for the elect by virtue of the blood and resurrection of Christ, and by a miracle of justice for those who will have refused up to the end grace and redeeming life.

Such is the answer given not by philosophy alone, but by Faith and Revelation, to the question we were led to ask a moment ago: In point of fact, will the aspiration of the human Person, of the entire man toward immortality remain forever unsatisfied? No, this aspiration will not remain unsatisfied, the soul and body will be reunited, this same Person, this identical human Person whom we knew and loved during our evanescent days, is actually immortal; this undivided human totality that we designate by a man's name will perish for a while, yes, and will know putrefaction; yet in reality and when all is said and done he will triumph over death and endure without end. And this immortality of Man is inextricably engaged and involved in the drama of the Salvation and Redemption.

V

I have a few words to add in conclusion. I should like to come back to some considerations that I touched on at the beginning of this essay, concerning the value of human life, that value which is greater than anything in the world, except things that are divine or concern what is divine in man, and serve, as Burke said, to redeem the blood of man — and such things, in truth, are not of the world, although they may be in the world.

Here we face a strange paradox, and the kind of assertion that may be — with the same words but according to diverse meanings — at the same time perfectly true and absolutely false. *Nothing in the world is more precious than human life:* if I think of the perishable life of man, this assertion is absolutely false. A single word is more precious than human life if in uttering this word a man braves a tyrant for the sake of truth or of liberty. *Nothing in the world is more precious than human life:* if I think of the imperishable life of man, of that life that will consist in seeing God face to face, this same assertion is perfectly true.

Human society can ask human persons to give and sacrifice their lives for it, as in the case of a just war. How is this possible? This is possible because the earthly common good of the earthly community is not a merely earthly good. Even this earthly common good involves suprahuman values, for it relates indirectly to the last end of men, to the eternal destiny of the persons who compose society. Human society must tend toward its earthly common good, toward a good and happy common life, in such a way that the pursuit of eternal happiness — which is more than happiness, for it is beatitude, and God himself — may be opened and made feasible for each human person in the community. If the common good of human society were only and exclusively a set of temporal advantages or achievements, as the common good of a beehive or an anthill, surely it would be nonsense for the life of a human person to be sacrificed to it.

In regard to human civilizations, or pseudo civilizations, two mortal errors are to be pointed out in this connection. A civilization which despises death because it despises the human person and ignores the value of human life, a civilization which squanders the courage of men and wastes their lives for business profits or for satiating covetousness or hate or for the frenzy of domination or for the pagan pride of the state, is not a civilization, but barbarism. Its heroism is heartless bestiality.

But on the other hand a civilization which knows the price of human life but which sets up as its main values the perishable life of man, pleasure, money, selfishness, the possession of acquired commodities, and which therefore fears death as the supreme evil and avoids any risk of self-sacrifice and trembles thinking of death, under the pretext of respecting human life — such a civilization is not a civilization, but degeneration. Its humanism is cowardly delicacy.

True civilization knows the price of human life but makes the imperishable life of man its transcendent supreme value. It does not fear death, it confronts death, it accepts risk, it requires self-sacrifice — but for aims that are worthy of human life, for justice, for truth, for brotherly love. It does not despise human life and it does not brutally despise death; it welcomes death when death, as pioneers and free men see it, is the accomplishment of the dignity of the human person and a beginning of eternity. Let me recall in this connection the words of the late Greek statesman, Mr. Metaxas, spoken to an American war correspondent. " We Greeks," he said, " being Christians, know that after all death is only an episode." An episode on the road of the immortal life of man. Such is Christian civilization, true civilization. Its heroism is genuine heroism, a heroism integrally human, because divinely grounded in the immortality of man.

3

THE IDEA OF GOD IN THE MIND OF MAN

Maude Royden

MAUDE ROYDEN (Mrs. Hudson Shaw), assistant preacher at the City Temple, London, from 1917 to 1920, was cofounder of the Fellowship Services at Kensington. She was active in the Women's Suffrage Society before the First World War, and edited its paper, *The Common Cause*. In 1930 she was made a Companion of Honor, and two years later received the degree of Doctor of Divinity from the University of Glasgow — an honor only once before granted to a woman.

3 *Maude Royden*

THE IDEA OF GOD
IN THE MIND OF MAN[1]

*M*AN MAKES GOD in his own image. It is indeed because he is in part divine that he knows there is a God at all. To know it is to know something that is true, and therefore it is rightly said that there is " truth in all religions."

As we move upward in the scale, our idea of God is proportionately exalted. We learn to know him better. Still, we know him only as we are capable of knowing him and still, inevitably, make him in our own image. Herbert Spencer, the Positivist, observed with something of a sneer that, if a triangle could think, it would think that God was triangular. Undoubtedly — but the sneer is gratuitous. If God exists and triangles exist, then triangularity must be included in the Godhead which created them. So, when man believes that God is Personal, he believes rightly. How could Personality exist if God had not created it? And how could God create what he had not in himself? To say that God is " a Person " is no doubt an error; to say that his Being includes Personality must be true.

In the temples of Shintoism there are no images of God. High up on the wall, but tilted so that the worshiper, looking upward, sees himself reflected in it, there is a looking glass. A Shinto priest explained this to me by saying that no believer can see more of the Godhead than is already in his heart; the

---

[1] Delivered at Lancaster, Pennsylvania, as the Garvin Lecture for 1942, under the title, " The Idea of God as Affected by Modern Knowledge."

mirror in which he sees only himself reminds him of this. Is it not the counterpart of our Master's teaching, when he said, " Blessed are the pure in heart: for they shall see God "?

The fact is that we do not think wrongly if we find in God certain human qualities. We err only when we imagine that our thoughts are adequate. This is the tragic error that has hampered progress and taught mankind the vices of intolerance and cruelty. This is what has made believers persecute those whose beliefs are unlike their own, claiming for themselves sole possession of the truth.

But all who have any religion at all have some part of the truth, however rudimentary. Even the animist and the fetishist have it. They believe in a spiritual power, unseen but real, and, since it is the essence of religion to believe this, they are " religious " and know something that is true.

Such " religion " is, however, superstitious, since everything that it teaches beyond that is false. It was not until the great spiritual faiths arose that man reached the nobler knowledge that a spiritual Power not only exists but is worshipful, and to be worshiped not solely for what can be got from it but for its own sake.

It may be truly said that every such religion has been part of the spiritual education of the human race, since each has taught us some aspect of the Divine that is true, though — like all human conceptions — necessarily inadequate. Egypt gave to us the idea of God as scientific Truth, Persia as Light or Purity, Greece as Beauty, Rome as Law, India as Spirit, Islam as Transcendence, Judaism as Righteousness.

Christianity centers its teaching — and to us Christians consummates all — in the conception of a God who is Love.

To claim that this revelation is final for humanity is not to bar the way upward or to suppose we now possess all knowledge. The Founder of our religion said, on the last evening of his life on earth, " I have yet many things to say unto you, but ye cannot bear them now," and since then not two thousand years have passed. Anthropologists suggest that the human race is at least a million years old. So short a space as two thousand years may well find us very primitive Christians still.

> God has other Words for other worlds,
> But for this world the Word of God is Christ.
> And when we come to die we shall not find
> The day has been too long for any of us
> To have fulfilled the perfect law of Christ.
> Who is there that can say " My part is done
> In this: now I am ready for a law
> More wide, more perfect for the rest of life? "
> Is any living that has not come short?
> Has any died that was not short at last? [2]

So, immediately, there is evident need for growth and for a new and ever loftier conception of God. Even before the canon of the New Testament was closed, the author of the Fourth Gospel interpreted the Christian faith to a second generation of Christians in terms colored by Greek thought. The Greek thought of that time and world had become an influence with ordinary men in much the same way that scientific thought has influenced the mass of us today. The rolling centuries have each left their mark on Christian theology and, where men have done their thinking honestly, our Lord's promise has proved true: " I have yet many things to say unto you, but ye cannot bear them now. Howbeit when he, the Spirit of truth, is come, he will guide you unto all truth."

The extent to which the love of truth has been rewarded by growing knowledge, and our idea of God ennobled by our increasing knowledge of his Creation, has not been realized with sufficient clearness. Therefore religious men have neither welcomed this knowledge nor understood its influence on theology. Perhaps it would be truer to say that the religious have fought against the light and the skeptical been dazzled by it; so that the theologian has condemned it as likely to induce

---

[2] Harriet Eleanor King, *The Disciples* (London, 1907), pp. 101-102. Reprinted by permission of Routledge and Kegan Paul, Ltd.

skepticism about the very existence of God, and the skeptic, in agreement for once with the theologian, has accepted the charge and ceased to believe.

Yet this has not been true of some of the greatest scientists, or the truly religious, for these latter have loved Truth as an aspect of the Divine, and the former, in some conspicuous cases, have proclaimed their faith in God:

I had rather believe all the fables in the Legend, and the Talmud, and the Alcoran, than that this universal frame is without a mind; and, therefore, God never wrought miracles to convince atheism, because his ordinary works convince it. It is true, that a little philosophy inclineth Man's mind to atheism, but depth in philosophy bringeth men's minds about to religion; for while the mind of Man looketh upon second causes scattered, it may sometimes rest in them, and go no farther; but when it beholdeth the chain of them confederate, and linked together, it must needs fly to Providence and Deity.[3]

" An undevout astronomer is mad," writes Edward Young, but the astronomer also speaks for himself. Johannes Kepler, as he watched through his telescope the motion of the stars in their courses, declared that he felt that he " was thinking the thoughts of God after him."

The discovery of even a small fragment of scientific truth produces on the discoverer an extraordinary sense of *exaltation.* Is this not to be explained by his having been the instrument of a revelation? He has not created anything, but it is in effect as if he had done so — had established a piece of irrefutable and eternal truth — had added one stroke to the grand picture of reality in this astounding universe. How eagerly should not religion have seized upon these great conquests of the human spirit and made them her own! And the loss to science — it is incalculable — that men of science should be afraid of religion![4]

In the light of utterances like these let us examine the effect of modern man's discoveries and achievements on his theology. It will be seen at once that in an age of great mechanical ad-

[3] Francis Bacon, *Essays* (London, 1867), p. 169.
[4] Professor Arthur Smithells, in a private letter.

vance a mechanical conception of God is natural. In the nineteenth century man made machinery of ever greater and greater
efficiency and of increasing power. So vast was his achievement in this direction that he fell down and worshiped the
thing that he had made. Machines that in the twentieth century
would seem hardly more than toys filled the men who first
made them with astonishment and awe. The principles on
which they were constructed worked with such magnificent
accuracy and power as to compel admiration and to be exalted
as an attribute of God himself. What could be more wonderful, more awful, than a great engine? Even now, when we
are more accustomed to the spectacle of gigantic power combined with exquisite precision — the classic example of the
steam hammer cracking a nutshell without injuring the kernel
is one of the least of these — it is impossible to look into the
engine room of a great steamship or the powerhouse of an
electrical generating station without seeing the beauty as well
as the might of such creations. The men who operate the machinery of modern times are converted into giants. One man
wields the strength of seventy thousand horsepower. There
is no intoxication greater than the sense of power, and how
should men, bred to the exercise of power on such a scale and
yet new to it, fail to find it divine?

So first of all the universe, and then the Creator of the universe, were converted in men's minds to a vast machine. This
mechanical universe operated as man-made machines do: it
was therefore powerful, exquisite and relentless. Everything
happened as it does with machinery and no room was found
for God except — in the minds of those unwilling to relinquish
religious belief altogether — as himself a sort of machine.

> Streams will not curb their pride
> The just man not to entomb,
> Nor lightnings go aside
> To give his virtues room;
> Nor is that wind less rough which blows a good man's barge.[5]

[5] Matthew Arnold, *Poetical Works* (London, 1929), p. 451.

The Almighty had made the universe, but as one makes a watch. He had wound it up and left it to itself. In course of time it would run down undoubtedly, and it remained an open question whether its Maker could or would wind it up again. If not, there would be an end of it.

The world however was not what mechanics thought it was; nor was its Creator. Man had once more made his god in his own image and, under the influence of further thought, began to doubt its truth.

The question of evolution began to exercise men's minds. Probably no great scientific hypothesis ever created so profound an impression so immediately as that of the origin of species, as set forth by Darwin. This was no doubt partly due to the fact that there was much intellectual curiosity abroad and men were in a questioning mood; it was even more directly due to a quality (which may be called accidental) in the mind of the man whose name will be forever associated with one of the most momentous discoveries of all ages. Charles Darwin was a man of singular intellectual humility. His worship of truth had in it no vestige of arrogance toward other men. He did not think of them as less endowed than himself either with the love of truth or with the ability to grasp it. He took very great pains to make his theory understandable by the laity. He wrote his book in clear, limpid and admirable English prose. Everyone who wanted to understand the theory of evolution could do so. It was a matter of taking trouble to read with care what Darwin wrote with care; and in that questioning age an unusual proportion of readers did so, influenced perhaps not only by intellectual curiosity but even by an unconscious response to the appeal of a great scientist who had taken trouble to be understood.

The Origin of Species became the Bible of nineteenth-century thought. It was treated exactly like a Bible; that is to say, it was read with critical judgment by some, with devout and almost idolatrous faith by others. It was quoted, without being read carefully, by thousands, and believed, without being read at all, by millions.

Darwin was an agnostic — a humble and devout agnostic. He was immediately called an atheist by people who were unable or unwilling to grasp the difference between a man who humbly admits that he does not know whether there be a God and a man who dogmatically pretends to know there is not. Yet Darwin's conception of the ways of God, whose existence he doubted, profoundly affected the theology of those who still believed. In spite of the indignant protests of Christians whose faith was based on a wholly fantastic conception of the verbal accuracy of every statement in the Bible, belief in the theory of evolution established itself. The first chapter of Genesis was no longer held to be a miraculously correct account of an event that was described with equally miraculous correctness in the second chapter, the two accounts differing in almost every detail: it was seen to be the version of a poet and a prophet, of the divine process of creation seen in evolution.

The obvious differences between these two accounts of the same event — the creation of the universe — did not trouble the writers or collaborators of the first and second chapters of Genesis, since they had no idea that future readers would suppose them to be writing an exact history. "Exact history" was a conception wholly unknown to them. All the writers knew was that these myths or legends contained truths that were well worthy to be set down and meditated on. Were they not right — as completely right as editors of the works of John Bunyan, who bound up in a single volume the two allegories familiar to us as *Pilgrim's Progress* and *The Siege of Mansoul* without being troubled by the fact that neither is "an exact history" of anything that ever happened to any individual Christian?

Without being guilty of irreverence, therefore, one may well point out that the first chapter of Genesis, which is a sublime poem, is much nobler than the second, which is a piece of picturesque and ancient folklore. In proportion to its noble beauty is its fundamental truth. How, one may well ask, could the hypothesis of evolution be more grandly stated than by this great unknown poet? The process of evolution as expounded by Darwin has been challenged, criticized and modified by other men of science; as set out by the author of Genesis 1, it stands forever. The poet is the greater exponent of fundamental verity.[6]

While scientists and theologians were engaged in furious controversy, the man in the street, captivated by Darwin's sweet reasonableness and cogent logic, was accepting this new hypothesis and adapting his theology to it. No longer bludgeoned by a false faith into a blind assent to everything that was " in the Bible," he began to consider whether the God who ordered bears to devour a band of small children, for the very minor offense of laughing at a good man with a bald head, was actually the God revealed to us by the Savior, whose love for children was so great as to have revolutionized our attitude toward them. The question had only to be put to be answered — no. What then? Must we dismiss as false the whole of the Old Testament? Again no. Its religious value and beauty make the very idea impossible. But let us consider it as an evolutionary document, in which is recorded the slow process of man's search for God.

I call the Bible a record of the search of man for God rather than a progressive revelation of the Divine, because the latter phrase suggests a certain unwillingness on the part of the Revealed One; but in fact both descriptions are true. The divine spirit breathed by the Lord God into man to make of him " a living soul " has never rested in its search for more and more knowledge of its Creator. The Bible records that fact. But always the God of Love after whom men have groped, " if haply they might feel after him and find him," has sought man

---

[6] This was said by Professor Arthur Thompson, himself a scientist.

and revealed himself, as the seeker was able to endure the Light. "No man hath seen God at any time," but the obstacle to our seeing has been in man, not in God.

It is impossible to overestimate the value of the work done by Biblical scholars on the Old and New Testaments. Released from a theory of "verbal inspiration" that paralyzed sincere criticism, they in turn have released us from the necessity of believing in a "jealous" and — even more important perhaps — a capricious God. It was not possible to reconcile (for example) the Deity who in anger drowned the whole human race, except eight persons, with him who found it worth while to be crucified for that same race, or who "so loved the world, that he sent his only begotten Son, that whosoever believed in him should not perish, but have everlasting life." But it is both possible and reasonable to see in this the record of man's better understanding of what is and what is not truly divine. This better understanding has not been a steady light; it has been, and it is, a flickering flame. It glows and increases, it faints and almost fails. But it has never gone out nor has the darkness overwhelmed it, since God made man a living soul.

Neither has God left himself without a witness. The theory of evolution has made possible a more reverent and a more realistic attitude to religions other than our own. The aspects of Deity proclaimed by them became available for us, modern and Western as we are, through the teaching of scientists rather than of theologians. It has greatly exalted our idea of God. Though men might always have believed that the Christian teaching, "God is Love," logically included all the rest, the supposed need for proof that, if Christianity is "right," all other revelations are "wrong" has narrowed our idea both of God and of Love. The idea that he is not also Truth as the ancient Egyptians taught, and Beauty as the Greeks believed, and Power and Righteousness as shown by Romans and Jews, has never — of course — been expressly denied. Did not Christ himself say that he was the Truth? But, while acknowledging this in a perfunctory way, the real thought of Christian people has been quite other. I should say for my own part that the suppression of the true and the suggestion of the false is the characteristic vice of the Christian churches. " Economy " of knowledge, refusal to admit error, moral cowardice in the face of advancing knowledge — these have been the outstanding defects of Christians. It is impossible here to quote the almost innumerable examples of this tragic weakness but it is also superfluous; they are only too well known. From the records of scientific discovery to those of Biblical criticism the Christian reader can only turn with feelings of disgust and shame. A Galileo, a Darwin or a Colenso proves to us the shameless disregard of truth with which theologians have too often combatted the advance of knowledge.[1] If we had not felt bound to condemn other religions as false, we should have given a nobler worship to a God who is Truth.

Another glaring instance is in our tendency to dissociate our idea of God from Beauty. It is true that this dissociation is so preposterous that, with Christians as with other worshipers, our loveliest and our noblest art has always been religious; but along with that has gone an ascetic contempt for Beauty and a tendency to regard it as a dangerous thing likely to " come between ourselves and God." To fear it as dangerous has been the fault of the Catholic ascetic, to despise it as meretricious that of the Protestant Philistine. St. Bernard drew the cowl over his face lest the loveliness of the Lake of Lucerne should distract his mind from God. To this day, conscientious worshipers cursed (or blessed) with a love of music tell me that they *cannot worship* in such and such a church " as the music there is so beautiful that it comes between them and God."

Would our insincere and sentimental church music, our deplorable hymn tunes, our meaningless architecture fashioned

---

[1] See Andrew D. White's *A History of the Warfare of Science with Theology in Christendom* (New York, 1907).

to imitate rather than create, have been possible if we had with heart and soul acknowledged the Lord as the First Author of Beauty? That we have also built glorious churches and cathedrals, composed sublime music and painted great pictures, cannot excuse these things or explain away the defense offered for singing a bad tune — " because we like it." A Greek in ancient days would have thought it as valid an excuse as to say that we may get drunk because we like alcohol. But the religion of Greece being " false," we dare not admit that Beauty is the most perfect expression of a God of Love. What indeed can create Beauty but Love?

The theory of evolution has set us free. We can now boldly interpret the great saying that God " left not himself without a witness " throughout the ages; the witness of poets and prophets of other faiths than ours can now be seen in its true aspect, as part of the spiritual education of the human race. Our God of Love takes up into himself Beauty and Truth and Power. Love is no longer sentimental. The Transcendence of the God of Islam and his Power, the Beauty of Greek religion and the Righteousness of Jehovah, the Purity of Zoroastrianism, the Immanence and Spirituality of the Hindu — all are ours to worship, and whatever more a widening conception of Love can give to the Christian of today.

We have traveled far from the strange habit of mind that permitted the creators of the great Authorized Version of the Bible to make St. Paul say, " Ye men of Athens, I perceive that in all things ye are *too superstitious*," when in fact he said, " In all things ye are very religious."

Let us have the whole passage: " Ye men of Athens, I perceive that in all things ye are very religious. For as I passed by, and beheld your devotions, I found an altar with this inscription, TO THE UNKNOWN GOD. Whom therefore ye ignorantly worship, him declare I unto you." [8] It is only of recent times

[8] Acts 17: 22-23.

that the average Christian could allow himself to say that the Unknown God of the "heathen" is the God he himself worships.

In gaining this freedom we have already gained a nobler thought about God and of what is meant by his Fatherhood. He could have made us slaves or puppets; he has made us sons. We have the freedom of friendship, and our Lord himself says to us, "Henceforth I call you not servants; for the servant knoweth not what his Lord doeth: but I have called you friends; for all things that I have heard of my Father I have made known unto you." How much more worshipful is such a God than one whose attributes are those of the unreasoning despot! How truly may we have boldness in access to him and with what reverence seek ever a further and further understanding of his purposes for us!

For this idea of God is forward-looking in its greatness. To see how Man has "felt after him and found him, . . . though he be not far from every one of us" is to be filled not only with humility at our blindness and stupidity, but with exaltation and hope. "Look unto the rock whence ye are hewn, and to the hole of the pit whence ye are digged." The rock whence we are hewn! We — who now are called to grow up to the measure of the stature of the fullness of Christ! How far we have to go — but how far also we have already come!

Natural science has yet another claim upon our gratitude. For submission to all-powerful but uncertain Deity it has offered us co-operation with an unchanging God.

This has been one of the hardest of all lessons to learn. We ourselves are capricious. To us the very idea of power is associated with freedom to be capricious. To change one's mind, to do so without being bound to offer (or to have) any reason, to favor one course and to reject another — this has seemed to us of the very essence of power. The servant must do what he is told, when he is told — but not the master. He may do as he likes, when he likes, simply because he chooses so. Caliban is not the only one who has admired and envied a god Setebos for his power to do just this. The tendency to attribute to God the senseless caprices that rule ourselves has been very common. But it has been an uneasy cult. We have been constrained to walk delicately with a God like this. He might assure us of his tender mercies toward us, but how should we know how long this mood would last? His ways are not our ways and we could never be sure of him. Our approach to his throne must always be made, like Esther's to Ahasuerus, in complete uncertainty as to our reception, whether for life or for death. Our prayers, whose efficacy, we have been taught to believe, depends on the degree of certitude with which we make them, must be offered to a God whose response is wholly uncertain. The Savior commanded us to pray but in such terms as these:

What things soever ye desire, when ye pray, believe that ye receive them, and ye shall have them.

And all things, whatsoever ye shall ask in prayer, believing, ye shall receive.

Whatsoever ye shall ask in my name, that will I do. [9]

These are hard sayings to those whose God is as uncertain a quantity as he has often been in our thoughts, and the position is not appreciably eased when we are assured that it was " better for us " that our prayers should be unanswered. This may very well be true, but why then did our Lord teach us that their efficacy depended on our conviction that they would be answered? If our difficulty arises from our uncertainty as to which prayers are and which are not in harmony with the will of God, it is necessary that we should know his will, and this we cannot do unless he is constant.

It is this constancy or trustworthiness of God to which science has led our faith. The idea that he is a relentless machine

[9] Mark 11: 24; Matthew 21: 22; John 14: 13.

has passed: it was too empty to hold us. But it has left us enriched. We are better able to think of God as trustworthy and changeless — though not with the cold impersonal changelessness of a perfect machine. His nature is lit up for us by the knowledge of scientific law.

The "laws" of science should be called by a better name. It is a misfortune that our English language uses but one word for two conceptions so exceedingly diverse as a statement of observed fact in nature and an act of Parliament. The result has been a confusion of thought which is one of the causes of our confusion of spirit. We know that a "law" promulgated by a ruler or a ruling body — a king, a dictator or a parliament — can be and often is broken. The offender may be caught and punished or he may escape, but he *can* break the law. There is no impossibility about it. And so, by a confusion of thought, he has believed that he can break the laws of God. But he cannot.

The laws of nature are not "laws" in the Parliamentary sense at all: they are statements of fact. If they appear to be "broken," we know that they have not been correctly stated. The "law" of gravitation might appear to such an observer as Einstein to be "broken," but he does not dream of recording any such absurdity. He knows that, if *his* observations are correct, those of Isaac Newton were not entirely so. This does not derogate from the greatness of Newton. What he observed he set down, and from it deduced a great "scientific law." It means only that, building on his foundation, an Einstein — as great a man and possibly greater — has seen farther, and more, and has enunciated another "law"; but nothing has been "broken."

It is true that there are still beings who suppose that, by touching wood, crossing fingers, walking under a ladder or breaking a looking glass, they can avert or create a misfortune. Most of them do not seriously believe it. Most of them are well aware that, if one turns on the gas, leaves it turned on and some time later lights a match, there will be an explosion that no amount of wood-touching will avert. They do not cross their fingers and then lay them on a live wire — being of opinion that, if they do so, they will infallibly be electrocuted. They know as well as the late G. K. Chesterton — though they may not phrase their knowledge so wittily — that " a man is free to throw himself over a precipice if he chooses but he will not break the law of gravitation if he does so: he will illustrate it." The most superstitious Christian knows these things and guides his actions more constantly by such knowledge than by his superstitions.

Moreover, the modern man has learned that, by obedience to laws he can neither evade nor break, he can become master of colossal forces. Gas, steam, electricity, water power, wind and gasoline — all these are his servants as long as he is their servant. By the most careful study and the most studious observance of the " laws " of nature he can " see " into universes and into the atoms that compose them. He can send his voice round the world and annihilate distance. He can conquer disease and make the desert blossom like a rose. And all this he can do because he has discovered that the " laws " of nature are not breakable, or capricious, but trustworthy.

This universe, the Christian believes, is the work of God. It must then reflect the mind and purpose of its Creator. He too must be trustworthy. Ages ago men learned this, and learned too to co-operate with the Creator and to profit by his co-operation:

And God said, This is the token of the covenant which I make between me and you and every living creature that is with you, for perpetual generations. I do set my bow in the cloud, and it shall be for a token of a covenant between me and the earth. And it shall come to pass, when I bring a cloud over the earth, that the bow shall be seen in the cloud: And I will remember my covenant, which is between me and you and every living creature of all flesh; and the waters shall no more become a flood to destroy all flesh.

And the bow shall be in the cloud; and I will look upon it, that

I may remember the everlasting covenant between God and every living creature of all flesh that is upon the earth.[10]

And again:

While the earth remaineth, seedtime and harvest, and cold and heat, and summer and winter, and day and night shall not cease.[11]

In the belief that " seedtime and harvest " would not cease, men sowed and in due time they reaped. But the full majesty of the spiritual law was not, at least in the West, realized, until it was irradiated for us by the conception of scientific law.

The success of what is called " Christian Science " has owed much to the distaste of the modern man for an incalculable deity. One who may answer our prayers for healing with a cancer or a recovery, and who expects to be praised for his mercy in either case, makes the faith he demands an impossibility. It is truly possible to say, " Though he slay me yet will I trust him," and many thousands of believers have said it and will continue to do so. " Let God be true though every man a liar." The devout will not shrink from the knowledge that there is something in them that stands between their prayer and God. Of Christ we are told at least once that " he could there do no mighty work, save that he laid his hands upon a few sick folk and healed them. And he marvelled because of their unbelief." But to be told that your prayer for life has been answered when the " answer " is death makes the prayer of faith impossible from the start. And how can it be said of a God who sends both health and disease that he is One from whom " every good gift and every perfect gift . . . cometh down," and " with whom is no variableness, neither shadow of turning "? Surely it was not a God of caprice who made the universe which science had revealed as one of majestic harmony and order?

[10] Genesis 9: 12-16.
[11] Genesis 8: 22.

The phrase, " Christ Scientist," though one may reject the edifice of belief that has been built upon it, and even think it in the last resort very unscientific, is a great phrase. It expresses a sense of the majestic order which prevails in the stars and in the atom. It expresses our faith in the constancy of the divine purpose and the unvarying character of God's laws. It has brought a radiant peace and calm to many a troubled soul.

To those who (like myself) are not Christian Scientists, the science they invoke has been a great revelation. We now see that our Lord was a profound realist, that his spirit was in the best sense scientific. Far from struggling against the light of knowledge it has brought us understanding and " set us free."

Consider the reputed " hard sayings " of Jesus Christ. I am thinking here not of practical hardness — hardness in practice — such as we all find in the fulfillment of his ideal ethics; but of a difficulty in understanding or justifying certain elements in his teaching. There are many such sayings. One, for example, is found at the close of the parable of the talents: " Unto every one that hath shall be given, and he shall have abundance: but from him that hath not shall be taken away even that which he hath." This, say indignant critics, is unfair. That is not the point. Our Lord is not giving an order but stating a fact. It is simply a *fact* that one who neglects to use a talent he possesses loses that talent, and another who works at it develops and increases it. No artist, no craftsman, would dream of denying such a statement of fact as this. But it is true of other " talents," such as wealth or friendliness or courage. The friendly man exercises his gift until his friends are legion. The brave man, by the very exercise of courage, grows braver. But the thin-skinned and unsociable, unless they try hard to develop that small gift of human kindliness with which they are endowed (as with one talent), become more and more isolated, and shrink more and more from the sociable contacts they often long to enjoy. Are these things not obvious? Is it not silly to argue about them? Our Lord, in calling attention to them, is, like the scientist, making a statement of fact, and no amount of argument about the justice of facts will make them anything but facts.

I have heard critics more anxious to find fault than to understand complain of the parable of the wise and foolish virgins. Those who bought no oil were no doubt foolish, they declare, but were nevertheless much less disagreeable people than those who brought oil and refused to share it. Folly is, after all, preferable to meanness. But this is folly indeed; for Jesus, here also, is dealing with truths that life proves to be facts, even if hard facts. What is the oil with which we feed our lamps to light our path? Clearly it is wisdom. But can wisdom be shared, as if it were a cake that can be sliced up and handed round? Or a cruse of oil into which every one can dip his measure and take his share? No — it is not of this nature. Wisdom is bought not with money but with life, with blood and sweat. No one can give it us: we must win it. The wisest and most loving parents can indeed advise their children from their own wisdom. They can, with their own lamps, shed a little light on the paths their children must tread. But that is all. The time will come when they would give their very eyes to share with their children the wisdom they have so dearly bought; and they cannot. They can only say, " Go, and buy for yourselves."

Is this not true? Does not every parent and guardian know that it is true? Our inability to share what life has taught us may be a hard fact but it is a fact. Christ is a realist.

It is this utterly realistic way of looking at life that makes his ethical, idealistic teaching so illuminating, so free from every taint of sentimentality. There is nothing arbitrary in a God so revealed. Yet it is only to those who know a little — however little — of scientific law that its whole significance comes home. The spiritual law, we learn, is as immutable as scientific law; its very immutability is our release. We can co-operate with the divine purpose since we can trust it to be the same, yesterday, today and forever. We can learn to understand it, at least in so far as it concerns our co-operation. We are called to be fellow workers with God, and it is no longer arrogance but obedience to believe that we can and must be so.

The wide difference between this scientific understanding of the purpose of God and the older approach to it in the ages before Christ can be seen in a comparison of the second and third chapters of Genesis with the last paragraphs of the Sermon on the Mount. The writer in the book of Genesis tells us that there was a certain tree planted in the Garden of Eden of which Adam and Eve were forbidden to eat because it was of a specially sacred character and belonged to God. When, in spite of warning, they did eat of it, God was angry with them and punished them.

In the fifth, sixth and seventh chapters of Matthew, Jesus laid down the sublime principles of conduct that we call the Sermon on the Mount. These principles are so lofty, so idealistic, that even Christians have rarely lived up to them, and many have secretly or openly thought them fantastic. At the close of the Sermon, the Evangelist records the parable of the houses built on rock and on sand:

> Whosoever heareth these sayings of mine, and doeth them, I will liken him unto a wise man, which built his house upon a rock: And the rain descended, and the floods came, and the winds blew, and beat upon that house; and it fell not: for it was founded upon a rock.
> And everyone that heareth these sayings of mine, and doeth them not, shall be likened unto a foolish man, which built his house upon the sand: And the rain descended, and the floods came, and the winds blew, and beat upon that house; and it fell: and great was the fall of it.[12]

Observe the difference: Christ does not say, as might the author of Genesis, " Sand is specially holy and belongs to God: if you build on it he will be angry with you and will destroy your house." He says in effect, " Sand is a bad foundation: if

---

[12] Matthew 7: 24-27.

you build on it your house will fall down." There is no suggestion here that God is angry, no suggestion of punishment; even,
it may be said, no suggestion of wickedness. We are told that
here are the sound principles of good building: if we defy them
we are fools. The principles stand, unaffected by our de-
fiance: the house falls down.

One can suppose that, if our Lord had happened to illustrate
his ethic from the garden and the fruit tree, he would have said:
" The fruit of this tree is poisonous. Do not eat it or you will
die." But again there would be no threat of punishment, none
of the anger of God. Nor is there any suggestion that in eating
of the poisonous fruit we should be " breaking " God's laws.
We cannot break them: we can only break ourselves against
them.

In moving from the merely mechanical idea of God to one
more vital and more true, we are able to see how his changelessness, instead of turning us into mere puppets or machines, does
actually set us free. Indeed it endows us with power and helps
us to see why we shall ultimately use forces as great in the
spiritual world as we have learned to harness to our use in the
material world.

We shall: it is the language of faith. Unfortunately, just as
we began to believe that the forces of nature were ours to command, and to use them to grow rich and prosperous, two things
happened. Nature proved more mysterious than we supposed,
and scientific leadership began to falter; and civilization broke
down in two world wars.

We found that we were unfit to control the monstrous
powers we had thought to tame so easily. They were more
dangerous than we believed. We supposed we had only to put
them into operation and all would be well. Instead it appears
that we have brought destruction into the world on a scale
more astounding than could have been the wealth we had intended to heap up.

We turn to the scientist and find him faltering. He is no

longer sure. There are depths beyond depths of strangeness in the universe, and he no longer promises us all the kingdoms of the earth and the glory of them. Meanwhile our world is crashing about our ears. To whom shall we turn?

It has been said that, as Christ was the Word of God for this world, so are lesser men — still great in a more limited sense — "words" for their age or country. The great word for the nineteenth century was Evolution. The great word for the twentieth century was spoken by Einstein, and it is Relativity.

The second word was implicit in the first. Though science had shown us a constant and trustworthy universe, it was nevertheless a universe in flux. Its processes might be orderly but they were evolutionary. The very word implies change.

And, as ever, men's idea of God changed too. Evolution was a word of power and it fascinated, it almost hypnotized, their minds. It seemed to explain everything, to justify everything. It was majestic. Could God himself be outside it? Could he have designed for his Creation a process so beneficent and have no share in it himself? Impossible! God himself must be in evolution.

The Absolute vanished. In a delirium of admiration for the hypothesis that explained so much, the religious man proceeded to apply it to his God. Like man and all Creation the Creator was in evolution. In the hands of Bergson the great I AM disappeared and was replaced by the I BECOME. Not Being but Becoming was the essential attribute of Deity. It was no longer our idea of it that was in evolution but the God about whom our ideas were centered. "For the Devil is the ghost of primitive man, and God is the unborn life of the world that is yet to be." [13]

It is pathetic that in all our striving, however sincere, we seem to be forever unable to distinguish our God from ourselves. One might have supposed that to a generation of men

---

[13] Kirsopp Lake, "Prayer," *Atlantic Monthly*, CXXXIV (1924), 167.

and women so well acquainted with the history of religions this failure would have been impossible. It has not been so. Men of distinguished intelligence and great learning fell easily into the trap; they evolved, and the process was both stimulating and hopeful. Why should not their God evolve also? The stage was set for the prophet of relativity. Albert Einstein is a man as modest and as sincere as Charles Darwin. He has proved, by his own exertions to make it clear, his desire that his discovery should be as well understood by the ordinary man as was the theory of evolution. It is not his fault that the theory of relativity is incapable of being grasped by the mass of us. It is the misfortune of many. We are not easily mathematicians. It is the more remarkable that such strenuous efforts to understand have been made by so many.

Being in no sense a mathematician I have resigned myself to the fact that, whether Einstein understands his theory or not, I shall never do so. I am the more impressed with the enormous interest that it has aroused in us all. It is true that Evolution was the master word of nineteenth-century thinking and Relativity of the twentieth. However dimly we apprehend its meaning we accept the fact of its importance. The fact that it is incomprehensible is no bar to our respect for it. It was beginning to be realized that physical science was, in the words of a physicist, "getting into a mess." Darwin's hypothesis had been so severely criticized that quite a number of ill-educated people really supposed that the whole conception of evolution had been abandoned. They were perfectly ready to abandon with it the hopes of " final good " it had inspired. They were equally ready to hear that physics — which had now become the center of scientific interest — was at fault, and that the theory of vibrations or " waves " need not now be studied, as it had been replaced by the quantum theory almost before it was born. It was taken for granted that each hypothesis destroyed the preceding one and, almost as readily, that it would be replaced in turn too speedily to make it worth while to study it.

Simultaneously, with the failing interest in the work of other scientists, came the birth of a new science — the science of men's minds, psychology. Psychologists, if they know their business, profess not to prove or to deny the existence of God, but only to explain how we came to believe in him. In the process, however, they have succeeded in convincing many that there is in fact no God.

The explanation of our search is found by them to be in our own wishes, our own fears. We are born into a terrifying world from the safety and warmth of our mother's womb. "When we are born we cry that we are come to this great stage of fools," says Lear. It is more likely that we cry because we are terrified. Soon, however, we learn that there is someone who can stand between us and hunger — our mother — and later that there is a strong presence which makes us feel secure — our father. In infancy, at least, the most modern child accepts its parents as divine!

But the time comes when the horrid truth bursts upon us. There are distresses from which even the strongest and kindest of parents cannot save us, pains they cannot ease, perplexities they cannot explain, questions they cannot answer. What then? Must we face the vast, unknown and terrifying universe without protection? We cannot. It is too frightful. We look around in terror. We look past that disappointing human father, and we decide that, beyond and above him, there is, because there must be, another and greater Father — a God, who has none of the alarming limitations of the human one, who is almighty, omniscient and all-loving. We believe in this God, this Father, not because he exists but because we need him. He must be; and he must be what we want him to be.

It is probably unnecessary to remind the reader that this "explanation," though it may fit some of the facts, certainly does not fit them all. No doubt, as we have already seen, men are apt to look for what they want to find and to find what they look for. There are religious people whose religion is an escape from harsh reality. I noticed with interest that, in a recent poll, a large number of those interviewed objected to sermons on the war because they expected to find in church " a spiritual escape." Life is terrifying enough to make us all search our hearts when psychologists invite us to reflect whether we have not indeed invented God and invented the sort of God we needed. It is necessary, however, to remember that the business of finding out why we believe in a Father-God has nothing to say to the question whether what we believe is true. And we must further ask whether it is possible to argue that the Teacher who taught the Fatherhood of God as the central and essential Truth was one who was peculiarly afraid of life. Whatever may be thought of Jesus of Nazareth, it is difficult to believe that he was afraid of anything. A sublime audacity is rather the salient quality with which he impresses us — a sublime courage which was both physical and moral. That he invented the Fatherhood of God because he dared not face life without him is too wildly improbable a theory to be worth discussing.

Nevertheless, the long delving of psychologists into the strange and devious ways of human thought has uncovered to us ourselves in many ways that have startled us. We are startled, we are even horrified — and yet again and again we are convinced. We are indeed led by our own wishes, when we think ourselves most judicial and sincere. We deceive ourselves and the truth is not in us, nor are our motives what we thought. Every honest man will admit that modern psychology has taught him much about human nature, especially his own. If he is wise he will withhold intellectual assent from some of the more astonishing generalizations made by certain psychoanalysts " blinded by their own excess of light "; but he will not deny that light has come and he will not resent the process of disillusionment. Who wants to be deluded? Who wishes to believe a lie, however flattering to himself?

But at first, at least, it was inevitable that the process of " debunking " our own intelligence and ourselves should shake all our conclusions. We had believed there was a God and that he was fatherly to us. If our motives for doing so could not bear examination, could we any longer believe in our God? The light that showed us our motives would perhaps, if we were honest, show us that we could not.

And then, into this perplexity, so deeply affecting our religious thought, came the shock of the First and then of the Second World Wars.

These events, in the intellectual and in the material worlds, have produced a profound disillusionment amounting to despair. What, men ask, is the use of all our intellectual struggle? Science has come to a dead end. We cannot any longer even understand what it is driving at. And in the meantime all it has achieved has been to enable us to destroy ourselves. Not one nation or civilization is now at stake but the human race — humanity itself. In former ages men could not do this frightful thing. Now it is evident to the most thoughtful of our race that they can. In former ages, if one war was sufficiently terrible and widespread, it could destroy a civilization and plunge a continent into darkness. What matter? Other civilizations would arise — perhaps had already arisen, in some other part of the globe. All was not lost when the Roman Empire fell. India hardly knew of it, and China probably not at all. Today it is no longer possible to conceive a war that is not a world war. The United States has, in the face of the infinite reluctance of the people, been dragged into the wars of 1914-1918 and of 1941. If the final catastrophe is not to be final in the literal sense of the word — wiping out a race of beings by the incredible scale of its mass murdering, by consequent famine and by pestilence to which the enfeebled body will offer no resistance — it will apparently not be because of the intelligence of man. That intelligence has brought about that ruin.

Where is now thy God?

The question is well asked. He has receded into the remote

distance. He has gone so far that we cannot understand him, so far that we can with difficulty hear his Voice. The universe has recovered its mysteriousness. After the promise of light shed on it by sanguine thinkers of the nineteenth century, thick darkness has supervened. We had believed God comprehensible because his universe was so, or so we thought. We were ready to co-operate with this trustworthy and intelligible Being and, always working with him and according to his laws, to make of the world an earthly paradise.

We have made of it a hell, and our scientific thinkers only echo our despair. They no longer know, they only guess; they have no answer and they expect none.

In the midst of this horror a despair of the human intelligence supervenes. Our evolutionary, contingent God disappears into the void. Instead, we are offered for our worship a God of whom it may truly be said that " clouds and thick darkness are the habitation of his throne." He, whose ways were always humbly admitted to be not our ways, has now become so " other " that the very attempt to understand him is reckoned an unpardonable arrogance; and we humans so full of depravity that we are well served by our suffering for the insolent attempt. Like another Lucifer, whose other name was the Star of the Morning, a scientific race has attempted to seize the knowledge and the power of Deity and, like Lucifer, has fallen headlong into the pit. All that is left to us is to abhor ourselves in dust and ashes.

Let my last paragraphs express a hope that I am unable to relinquish. It is true that the rapid progress of scientific discovery in the nineteenth century induced a mood of optimism that is now seen to be a false dawn. It is true that certain theologians of the shallower sort assumed too easily that they " knew God " and could tell us that he " was a good fellow and 'twould all be well." It is true that we have made a mess of things. Was our optimism after all more shallow than the pessimism that has succeeded it? The men of the nineteenth century were, on the whole, optimistic, because those who were articulate were, on the whole, prosperous and comfortable. To such, optimism is easy and the belief that in the next world, as in this one, " 'twould all be well," very natural. The twentieth century sees its hopes confounded and the world going down into a hell of poverty, servitude and sorrow. For its children pessimism is as natural as was optimism to their grandsires. Is it more reasonable? I do not think so.

It was time that we felt ourselves less at ease in Zion and time that we realized the " otherness " of God. He is not merely immanent in us and all things — and we almost as good as he! — but transcendent and beyond our finding out. The adorable " baby Jesus " of the second chapter of Luke, and the compassionate Man who shared our griefs and pains, had too much banished from our religious consciousness the Incarnate Word of God, the Christ of the first chapter of John. In our Christian faith God had become Man so entirely that we had almost forgotten that he is Unknowable, Infinite, Absolute, Transcendent, to be described only in negatives because of our inability to conceive him.

But must we forever rush from extreme to extreme? Must we now forget the Incarnation or think of God as the great Unknown? It is true that our human intelligence can understand but little of Deity; it is not true that we can understand nothing. To what purpose did our God become incarnate in the form of a Man if it were not that, in at least one of his aspects, we should learn to understand him? We cannot plumb his purpose for the universe, but we can and we must understand his purpose for ourselves.

Science is not bankrupt. It has taught us much. We have learned from it that we cannot " break " the laws of nature, but we have also learned that, if we co-operate with them in submission, we can do great things. We have to go forward to the knowledge that we cannot break the laws of God; but may we not also learn no longer to break ourselves against them?

Is this too much to hope for the followers of the Savior who told us how to live and warned us that, if we disregarded these principles, we should be as men who built upon the sand; but also that, if we observed and obeyed them, our house, built on the rock, would stand? Great as are the names of some of the theologians — a Karl Barth, a Reinhold Niebuhr — who, in the face of the darkness of the times, have warned us of our extreme wickedness and inability to understand God, I submit that to cast away the gains of scientific thought because we have misused science to our destruction is to despair too easily. God is still Immanent as well as Transcendent. He is still Christ as well as Jehovah.

We have learned to regard with reverence the teaching of all the great faiths of the world. Each has made its contribution, but broadly speaking it may be said that the genius of the East has been spiritual and that of the West scientific. All the living religions in the world today were born in Asia, and of India — which is the very heart of Asia — it may be said that her genius has been pre-eminently religious. This religious genius has grasped the changelessness of God and the inviolability of spiritual law, with a depth of conviction that is startling to us Westerners. The " fatalism " of Islam, the " karma " of Hinduism and Buddhism are born of this certainty. Believers in these religions do not suspect their God of caprice or expect from him any swerving from his righteous purpose. Absolute submission to the divine will or the divine order is of the essence of their faith. In this the Westerner is by comparison a child. He still imagines too readily that prayer is a means of changing the will of God to make it coincide with his. He is apt to " besiege the throne of God with prayer " and to regard the answer to his petition as a concession wrung from an unwilling Deity. I do not suggest that this crude and childish belief is unknown in the East or universal in the West; that would be absurd. I do suggest that it is much more common in the West and is even regarded as peculiarly religious.

The Easterner, however, has the defects of his qualities. His submission to the will of God is apt to become fatalism, his realization that he cannot hope to alter it apt to degenerate into despair. What we have called "progress" in the West has been erratic and even disastrous, but it may amend its ways and find its goal, while resignation is hopeless because it does not move at all. In Palestine, during the First World War, British engineers sent down the death rate among children in spectacular style by bringing clean water from the hills in a pipe line, whereas Moslems for centuries had acquiesced in their deaths as the will of God.

The scientific triumphs of the Westerner have been primarily due not to a desire for material comfort but to a noble and disinterested thirst for knowledge. Its disasters have been due to a greedy materialism, and the reverse side of the Western genius has been a vulgar worship of success. But if we give homage to the spiritual genius of the East we are also bound to see the best qualities of the West; and the disinterested love of Truth which inspired an Isaac Newton, a Darwin, an Einstein and a Marie Curie is such a quality. They have shown us immutable law in the material world, as the saints of the Orient in the spiritual; but they have done more. They have shown that it is the very presence of immutable order that makes possible achievements that are magnificent. They have not found in the laws of Nature a pious excuse for doing nothing and calling it submission to the will of God. They have found in it freedom and power. They have revealed to us a new and glorious meaning in the words, "whose service is perfect freedom."

How noble a world will be made when the genius of the East and the genius of the West, spiritual and scientific, are united — when to the Oriental sense of the immutability of law is joined the Western sense that in such immutability is found the groundwork for co-operation and achievement! Here lies our way. The intellectual victories won in the past must not be discounted because they have been abused. They must be controlled and guided by spiritual insight. Their prostitution to the production of material luxury must disappear. When the spirit of Christ takes control, the intellect becomes the handmaid of that spirit, and uses it in the service not of the few who have too much but of the many who have too little. The tragedy of war already offers an opportunity, and, when it ends, the opportunity will be colossal. All our brains will be needed to cope with the world's problems of feeding, clothing, healing and organizing for peace; but all will again go astray, as in 1918, if the intelligence of mankind is used to exploit and domineer rather than to love and serve.

Our Savior was born in Asia, as were all the great Founders of religions — but on the very edge of Asia, in Palestine, whose face is toward Europe. Through that little country ran the great highways that linked Europe and Asia with Africa. It was at the center of the known world that Jesus Christ was born. Was that mere accident? Is it not, at the least, a symbol?

In him the profound spirituality of the East is united with the scientific genius of the West. In him religion becomes no longer a retreat but a redemption — a victory. Like the greatest of Oriental teachers he sees the Spirit in all things and in it true reality: " God is Spirit." But the material is neither intrinsically evil nor a mirage. It too expresses God (" Consider the lilies of the field, how they grow ") and it too is holy, for it is sacramental.

Since we must think even of God with human thoughts because we have only human minds to think with, it is clear that our idea of him must forever be utterly inadequate. For the same reason we must think of God with *all* our mind and all its strength. Neither East nor West nor South can be left out, and the spiritual experience of no race must be left unused. It is good that our material successes in the West should have met with humiliating defeat, not only on the battlefield but elsewhere, for we had become arrogant and insanely satisfied with ourselves; but it is not good to cast away all that we have learned of the nature of God himself from the wonders of his Creation. It is not good that we should forget, even when we see the Lord " high and lifted up " and his train filling the temple, that his Son has called us not slaves but friends.

For this commandment which I command thee this day, it is not hidden from thee, neither is it far off. It is not in heaven, that thou shouldest say, Who shall go up for us to heaven, and bring it unto us, that we may hear it, and do it? Neither is it beyond the sea, that thou shouldest say, Who shall go over the sea for us, and bring it unto us, that we may hear it, and do it? But the word is very nigh unto thee, in thy mouth, and in thy heart, that thou mayest do it.[14]

[14] Deuteronomy 30: 11-14.

4

PSYCHICAL RESEARCH AND THE LIFE BEYOND DEATH

Hornell Hart

HORNELL HART is professor of sociology at Duke University. He was in charge of measuring changes in social attitudes for President Herbert Hoover's Committee on Social Trends. A member of the British and American Societies for Psychical Research, he has written *Personality and the Family*, *Skeptic's Quest*, *Can World Government Be Predicted by Mathematics?*, and other books and articles.

4 *Hornell Hart*

PSYCHICAL RESEARCH
AND THE LIFE BEYOND DEATH[1]

O UT OF THE billions of people on this earth there is just one whom you call " I." This strangely unique self of yours inhabits a physical body which is destined to die. Sooner or later, in some hospital room, or on the pavement of some highway, or in swirling waves, or in your bed at home, your body will go limp for the last time. Your heart will cease to pump blood through your brain. Your corpse will be dead. But what of the strange uniqueness that has said " I " within that body for all these years? Will it flicker out forever like a gutted candle flame? Or will that selfhood of yours go on in wider worlds, into vaster adventures?

This is no simple issue. It cannot be easily decided. We must search deeply if we would find foundations on which to build a rational belief about the problem of human immortality. The materialists do have what seems to them a simple and conclusive answer. They point out that personalities seem to be closely dependent upon their physical bodies and their physical brains. A baby develops intelligence only as his brain matures. The youth acquires knowledge as nerve currents reach his brain from his physical sense organs. If caffein reaches the brain the consciousness becomes alert, stimulated, intense. If alcohol flows through the bloodstream into that brain the per-

[1] Delivered at Lancaster, Pennsylvania, as the Garvin Lecture for 1943, under the title, " The Immortality of Man."

79

sonality undergoes the alterations of drunkenness. If a tumor destroys a portion of the brain a corresponding portion of the personality is altered. If the brain becomes diseased by syphilis the personality deteriorates. If the brain becomes aged the personality becomes senile. How then — if the brain be destroyed by the death of the body shall not the personality and its consciousness disintegrate forever?

But wait! Granted that the physical body and its brain do provide the matrix around which the personality grows up, and through which the personality expresses itself in the physical world — does that mean that destruction of the body must destroy the personality? Let us imagine a boy who has had all his music lessons and all his practice on one piano. Let us suppose that an accident to that piano breaks every third string and throws the remaining strings chaotically out of tune. If the boy then sits down to play he will be able to produce only broken discords. But do these discords prove that the musical personality of the player has been destroyed by the accident? Similarly, if the brain is destroyed, does that prove that the personality that has used this brain as its instrument has been destroyed?

Methods of Inquiry into Immortality

Destroyed by death or released by death into wider worlds? The answer is not obvious or easy. The problem has concerned mankind for tens of thousands of years. A great variety of methods have been used in seeking an answer. Some people quote the Bible as their final authority for the reality of the life beyond death. But, although the Bible is a significant part of the testimony that must be studied, we shall not offer it here as a basic proof of immortality. Some philosophers seek to prove eternal life by pure, abstract logic. We too shall seek to use logic, but we shall try to keep it closely related to facts and experiments. Some people use poetry and literary eloquence to set forth their own inner, intuitive assurance of life beyond death. Now poetry and strong inner conviction have their proper place, but of course they do not constitute proof for or against the reality which we together are seeking to test. Neither arbitrary authority, nor dogma, nor mere logic, nor unsupported intuition will serve our need for a trustworthy answer to this enigma of the ages.

Rather, we shall appeal to science. We shall not obtain any ultimate or absolute answer, for science always deals with probabilities, not with absolute proofs. In part of our inquiry we shall reach certitudes as high in probability as those accepted in such sciences as biology or geology, or even higher. At other points we shall have to weigh rival theories, and seek for evidence that may show us which are the strongest probabilities on which to build our purposes and our hopes.

The Fact of Extra-Sensory Perception

The first contributory problem upon which we shall seek scientific light is that strange group of phenomena called " extra-sensory perception." This group includes such reported occurrences as telepathy, clairvoyance, precognitive flashes of the future, and other weird events reported by various students in this field. What, then, is the scientific way of approaching this problem?

One of the first facts a modern scientist must accept is that it is impossible for him to repeat all of the experiments and all of the detailed and systematic observations that have been carried out by all the researchers who have preceded him. The modern scientist seeks to catch up with his predecessors as swiftly as possible and then to go on from where they left off. To do this he uses as a main springboard some basic textbook or group of textbooks that gather together, up to date, the established results of scientific research in a given field. Such a text is often called " a definitive study of the subject."

In the field of extra-sensory perception, if we were to attempt to repeat all the observations and the experiments of the pioneers and of the growing body of scientific students of the subject, we should never be able to get started on any fresh progress. There are literally hundreds of volumes of reports of scientific investigations and of proceedings of learned societies of psychical research that we should have to study, and whose decades of complex work we should have to repeat. What we need is a definitive work upon extra-sensory perception, a summary to bring together all the sifted results of the past and to provide us with a foundation upon which, after we have tested it, we may build a trustworthy superstructure.

Fortunately such books are available. If this lecture had been delivered forty years ago we might have turned to the two-volume study by Frederick W. H. Myers, published in 1903, under the title *Human Personality and Its Survival of Bodily Death*. If we had been starting out on the subject several years ago we might have used as our definitive text G. N. M. Tyrrell's *Science and Psychical Phenomena*, published in 1938. But since we are making our inquiry today we can begin far ahead of these older starting points. In 1940 a group of scientists, under the lead of Dr. J. B. Rhine of Duke University, brought together into one volume all of the important findings of all the scientific studies that had been made of telepathy and clairvoyance. They called their book *Extra-Sensory Perception after Sixty Years*.

This definitive study summarizes the results of 142 different investigations, in which over 3,600,000 tests were carried out. It tells of research reports in this field made by forty-eight different psychologists, who have used twenty-seven college and university laboratories in making their investigations. Having presented this monumental volume of research material, the book considers exhaustively and minutely the arguments against telepathy and clairvoyance. It reviews each of the hypotheses that have been offered as alternatives to extra-sensory perception. Persons who had criticized the telepathy hypothesis were urged to submit full statements of their objections, and these are presented in the book. The conclusion is clearcut. The probabilities are overwhelming that the results of these millions of tests are not due to mere chance. None of the other orthodox hypotheses presented by critics account for the results. The hypothesis of direct perception, beyond the physical senses, is the only valid explanation that thorough scientific study has been able to offer.

Those who propose to inquire into the question of human immortality by the methods of science are under obligation to consider carefully and thoroughly the findings of this book. Only if one can produce adequate evidence in refutation of the studies reviewed in such works as *Extra-Sensory Perception after Sixty Years* has one any scientific basis for rejecting telepathy, or for denying the other forms of extra-sensory perception. The reality of telepathy and clairvoyance has been established to a degree of probability higher than that which supports many propositions that are accepted generally as scientifically demonstrated in biology and geology.

It is true that not all scientists accept the reality of extra-sensory perception. As recently as 1940 the *Scientific Monthly* published an article by Sumner Boyer Ely which concluded as follows:

There has never been any evidence produced which would warrant the belief that there is such a thing as telepathy. . . . We can positively say that no mind has ever yet communicated with another mind other than through ordinary sensory channels. [2]

The author of the denial just quoted is the smoke inspector of Pittsburgh. From 1920 to 1940 he was professor of Commercial Engineering at the Carnegie Institute of Technology. In his own field he certainly deserves to be called a scientist. But

[2] Sumner Boyer Ely, " Telepathy, a Survey," *Scientific Monthly*, L (1940), 171.

when he asserts that telepathy has never yet occurred he claims to have proved a universal negative. He thus violates one of the fundamental logical principles of science. All the arguments that are basic in his article have been considered, thoroughly and dispassionately, by specialists in the fields involved, and these scientists reverse the verdict pronounced by Smoke Inspector Ely.

Of course, Professor Ely is not the only doubter of extra-sensory perception. Another type of objector is represented by John Mulholland in his book, *Beware Familiar Spirits*, published in 1938. His discussion of Dr. Rhine's work is very brief and superficial, but he does bring forward expert evidence to show that great numbers of stage performances that are supposed to be based on telepathy are actually produced by clever trickery. Now the stage presentations which claim to be telepathic are actually too successful to be trustworthy. Most of the results obtained in laboratory experiments achieve extra-sensory perception only irregularly, and usually incompletely. The same is true of most of the spontaneous cases trustworthily reported. The laboratory results usually prove to be significant only when averages of large numbers of cases are analyzed. There is no evidence in scientific studies for the belief that anyone on the stage can make the consistent hits throughout performance after performance, week in and week out, that stage imitations of telepathy present.

We are ready now to register certain conclusions about extra-sensory perception. First, telepathy is often faked in playful and even fraudulent ways, on the stage and elsewhere. Second, a good many persons of scientific training who have not thoroughly examined the full body of scientific evidence in the field have hastily and superficially denied the existence of extra-sensory perception. Third, telepathy and certain related phenomena do actually occur. That telepathy and clairvoyance exist has been demonstrated by scientific experiments in many countries over the past sixty years and more, which have proved over and over again that minds do come into contact with minds and with the outer world by channels other than the known senses.

The Meaning of Extra-Sensory Perception

What, then, is the meaning of this strange thing called extra-sensory perception, which this long series of scientific studies has so firmly established? This lecture hall is not a laboratory. Yet I propose to invite you to participate in an experiment for the purpose of making clear just what are the basic elements in the two major forms of extra-sensory perception. If you are willing to join me in this experiment, let me ask you, right now, to place each of your feet flat on the floor. Let your hands fall loosely on your thighs. Take as comfortable a position as you can. Now close your eyes and begin to relax. Let your hands grow heavier and heavier — utterly limp and relaxed. Let the muscles of your face grow heavier and heavier, completely at rest and limp. Now, while your whole body grows heavier and heavier and sinks into deeper and deeper peace, I want you to turn your attention to some place away from here where there is someone you love. Imagine that loved person as vividly as you can. Imagine his or her surroundings vividly. Imagine yourself as standing in front of that person, talking with him or her. Ask some question, and listen for that person to answer.

Now, if you have completed this inner experiment, please open your eyes, and let us discuss various aspects of it together. First, let us note that when you closed your eyes and relaxed you were shutting out of your consciousness part of that portion of your experience that comes to you directly through your sensory nerves and your voluntary muscles. Let us call that part of our experience " the sensori-motor world," or, simply, " the physical world." If each of us went into a completely dark room, absolutely insulated from all sound and from all disturbing vibrations, and if in such a room we relaxed completely in an absolutely comfortable reclining chair, we could approach fairly closely, for the time being, to excluding the sensori-motor world entirely. But we could still remain conscious, even with the sensori-motor world shut out. We could still remember the past; we could still plan for the future; we could still imagine; we could still dream; we could still think through the multiplication table, or engage in other abstract reasoning. And we could still have flashes of intuition. Let us call these parts of consciousness that could still continue — even when we relaxed in our utterly dark and quiet room — let us call these the " inner world." This inner world, then, would include memory, planning, imagination, dreams, abstract thought and imageless intuition.

When, in carrying out our experiment, you imagined yourself standing in the presence of some absent loved one, you were operating and observing in your inner world. Your focus of consciousness moved, from its usual imagined location within your physical head, into a location inside the head of your imagined body, standing in front of your imagined loved one, in the place in which the imagined form of your loved one was located. So far we are dealing merely with ordinary imagination. But let us combine this ordinary imagination with clairvoyance and telepathy. Suppose that when you carried out our experiment of a moment ago you had possessed a fairly high degree of clairvoyance. In that case, when you thought of your loved one at a distance, you would have perceived, not a mere imagined scene, but a more or less accurate vision of your loved one and of his or her surroundings, without having to see them with your eyes, touch them, or come into contact with them in any other physical way.

More familiar to the general public is that form of extra-sensory perception called telepathy. Let us assume, for illustration, that both you and your distant friend had the power of telepathy to a high degree. In that case, when you thought of your loved one, he or she would be aware of your thought. You would each be able to perceive to some extent what was in the mind of the other. Your two imaginations, plus your clairvoyant perception, would combine into one shared vision in which you would be able to see each other in the inner world, and to hear each other speak and reply. If your loved one had the psychological propensity to project this inner-world image into his or her physical surroundings, he or she would perceive you as an apparition. Once we accept extra-sensory perception as a fact, therefore, all we have to do is to combine that with the well-known facts of imagination and of projection of imagined images into the outer world, and we have a new phenomenon — namely, an apparition of a living person at a distance.

What we have thus theoretically recognized as possible has, as a matter of fact, been reported persistently in all ages and among all peoples. Among the members of this audience there are undoubtedly a number of persons who themselves, at one time or another, have actually perceived such apparitions. Indeed, the experience is reported so often that a group of British scientists, in 1889 to 1892, conducted a kind of poll in which seventeen thousand persons were interviewed. For every thousand persons questioned there were twenty-one reports of having seen realistic apparitions of persons who were still alive, and ten reports of having seen realistic apparitions of persons who were dead.[3] Apparitions of the living were thus seen just about twice as often as apparitions of the dead.

One of the cases reported in an earlier census of this sort is worth presenting here. The following account is abridged from a written statement by Rev. P. H. Newnham:

In March, 1854 [he reported], I was up at Oxford, keeping my last term. One evening, about 9 p.m., I flung myself, without undressing, on the bed, and soon fell asleep.

I then had a singularly clear and vivid dream, all the incidents

[3] *Society for Psychical Research Proceedings*, X (1894), 43.

of which are still as clear to my memory as ever. I dreamed that I was stopping with the family of the lady who subsequently became my wife. On arriving in the hall (on my way to bed) I perceived that my fiancée was only then near the top of the staircase. I rushed upstairs, overtook her on the top step, and passed my two arms round her waist, under her arms, from behind.

On this I woke, and a clock in the house struck 10 almost immediately afterwards.

So strong was the impression of the dream that I wrote a detailed account of it next morning to my fiancée.

Crossing my letter, not in answer to it, I received a letter from the lady in question (saying): "Were you thinking about me, very specially, last night, just about 10 o'clock? For, as I was going upstairs to bed, I distinctly heard your footsteps on the stairs, and felt you put your arms round my waist." [4]

DOES THE SOUL EXIST?

Not only have extensive censuses established the fact that modern people frequently perceive apparitions of the living, but the study of historical records shows that such apparitions have been reported in generation after generation. Moreover, the study of ethnology shows that, among almost all the primitive peoples who most closely approximate to the cultural status of our prehistoric ancestors, the seeing of apparitions has been accepted as real. [5] Not only primitive peoples, but also the great masses of believers in the religions of China, India, the Near East and Christendom, have held beliefs in the soul similar to the conception found by anthropologists to prevail widely in the primitive world.

Yet, in our own generation, behavioristic psychologists have disposed of the belief in the soul by a very simple method. They have merely asserted that nothing except the sensori-motor

[4] Edmund Gurney, Frederick W. H. Myers and Frank Podmore, *Phantasms of the Living* (New York, 1886), I, 225-226.

[5] Edward B. Tylor, *Primitive Culture* (New York, 1903), I, 417, 428, 429. Cf. Franz Boas, *Religion and the Future Life*, edited by E. Hershey Sneath (New York, 1922), p. 15.

world is real to science. Obviously those who confine their knowledge of reality to the physical world cannot know the soul, for by definition it transcends the sensori-motor realm. If the soul exists at all it functions in the world of consciousness and of purpose, of which the behavioristic psychologists profess to be so ignorant. Rather than accept their dogmatic prejudgment of the essential issue, let us state the problem in such a way that we can arrive at an answer scientifically.

The crucial question relative to the existence of the soul is this: Can the focus of consciousness observe and operate apart from the physical body? The essential test here rests upon the question of whether telepathy and clairvoyance can take place at a distance. Carefully controlled experiments have been made in extra-sensory perception at distances ranging from a quarter of a mile to over two thousand miles. It has been shown there is no relation between distance and success.[6] This means that minds do, under certain circumstances, observe what occurs in other minds and in the outer world apart from the physical body of the observer.

This demonstrated fact, that the focus of consciousness of certain persons can actually observe at a distance from the physical body, does, then, lay the foundation for acceptance of some form of belief in a soul. We begin to see more clearly the connection between this basic demonstration and the worldwide beliefs of mankind when we consider the apparitions that should theoretically occur if extra-sensory perception were combined with various forms of imagination, and of which actual reports come in persistently from points widely scattered over the earth.

The level of proof of these accounts of apparitions is not so high as the level of proof that has been attained for extra-sensory perception as a laboratory fact. Dr. Rhine himself holds

---

[6] J. B. Rhine, C. E. Stuart, J. G. Pratt, B. M. Smith and J. A. Greenwood, *Extra-Sensory Perception after Sixty Years* (New York, 1940), pp. 91, 97, 305.

that the reality of telepathy, clairvoyance and certain other forms of extra-sensory phenomena has been established, but he is very cautious about going beyond the laboratory facts. When one deals with reports of apparitions one has difficulty in making sure that the experience really occurred in the way in which it was reported. Sometimes such stories are deliberate hoaxes. Sometimes a partly real experience is exaggerated, consciously or unconsciously. Sometimes the will to believe adds untrue details that seem to make the event significant, or leaves out damaging facts that might destroy its value.

Psychical researchers have developed methods for guarding against these and other sources of error. The cases that have chiefly influenced the main conclusions of this lecture have been tested in various ways to insure their genuineness. But we must remember that the crucial proof of the existence of the soul is the fact of extra-sensory perception, and that this fact has been proved repeatedly in many laboratories. Since telepathy and clairvoyance do actually occur, we should normally expect that apparitions would be experienced. The reported cases of actual apparitions thus simply confirm the basic proof, and offer clues that point the way for further research.

" But," someone is going to argue, " are not apparitions just hallucinations? Some people do think they see them, of course. But aren't they mere delusions, which have no reality except in the inner mind of the person who thinks he sees them?"

That is exactly the point. If telepathy and clairvoyance are real we should expect apparitions of the living to occur that would be not mere delusions of the seer but real projections of the personality of the appearer. And we actually find reports of various kinds of proof that such self-conscious apparitions do actually take place.

Let us review briefly a sampling of this confirmatory evidence. The young lover already referred to, who embraced his fiancée even though his physical body was miles away, obtained confirmatory evidence in a letter from her which crossed his letter in the mail, and in the fact that both of these two letters told independently about the same apparitionally shared experience.

A second illustration is as follows. On March 22, 1884, at twelve o'clock at night, Mr. S. H. Beard, a member of the London Stock Exchange, deliberately attempted to project an apparition of himself into the presence of his friend, Miss L. S. Verity. He took the precaution of posting in advance, to a psychical researcher, a letter announcing what he intended to do. Eleven days later, on April 2, when he called upon Miss Verity in his physical body, she volunteered the information, without any suggestion on his part, that she had seen the apparition of him at about midnight on the night when he tried the experiment. She thereupon dictated and signed a statement describing her experience.[7]

A third illustration is the case of Alma Radberg, who was hypnotized by some experimenters in Sweden, and instructed to make an extra-sensory visit, in a distant city, to the home of one of the men present. She immediately brought back a circumstantial account of what this man's wife was doing at the time. A written record of what she said was made at once. Subsequently the wife confirmed in detail what the hypnotized girl had seen, and a written record of her confirmation was filed.[8]

The fourth illustration is an experience of Mr. M. Gabrielle Delanne in which he seemed to be standing outside his own body. He found himself able to move through a solid wall into an adjoining apartment where he had never been in his physical body. He inspected the rooms, fixed the remembrance of them in his mind, and noticed particularly the titles of some

[7] Gurney, *Phantasms of the Living*, I, 108-109.

[8] *Society for Psychical Research Proceedings*, VII (1891-1892), 205-206; VIII (1892), 405-406.

books on a shelf. After returning to his normal consciousness he secured admission to the apartment, and confirmed in detail what he had perceived clairvoyantly.[9]

We need much more and better evidence of the kinds just cited. But the data already collected tend to confirm what we should expect if and when telepathy and clairvoyance are combined with dreams, imagination and hypnotism.

Judging from the four cases that have just been presented, an apparition of a living person may depart from its physical body in a number of different ways. In the case of the student who embraced his distant fiancée, a vivid dream was the means of travel. A number of other cases are on record of apparitions seen at places of which the appearer was dreaming. In the case of Mr. Delanne, who left his physical body to visit the neighbor's apartment, a special type of dream or vision was involved, in which the excursionist perceived himself as being outside his own body. Many other cases of this kind also are on record. Such experiences are sometimes called " astral excursions." A third reported method of leaving one's body is through hypnotism. A fourth method consists in deliberate concentration of attention by an individual upon the purpose of projecting his apparition to some distant place, as was done by Mr. Beard in his appearance to Miss Verity. William James reported that a colleague of his on the Harvard faculty also succeeded in an attempt of this kind,[10] and other instances are on record.[11]

We have reviewed a very few of the innumerable cases in which apparitions of living persons have been perceived at a distance from their physical bodies, and in which the one whose apparition was perceived remembered later the experiences

[9] Quoted from M. Gabrielle Delanne's *Evidence for a Future Life* in C. W. Leadbeater's *The Other Side of Death* (Adyar, Madras, India, 1928), pp. 327-330.

[10] Walter F. Prince, *Noted Witnesses for Psychic Occurrences* (Boston, 1928), pp. 30-31.

[11] *Society for Psychical Research Proceedings*, XXI (1933), 223-228.

encountered in his excursion. Taken all together, such cases confirm the findings of laboratory experiments in extra-sensory perception. They show that not only can some minds perceive correctly the designs on shuffled cards inaccessible to their senses, and perceive correctly also the standardized card patterns thought of by some other mind; but some minds can occasionally enter into fairly full communication with other minds at long distances from the physical body, and can perceive and remember the surroundings and the events of the meeting.

We are therefore ready to define operationally the human soul. The soul consists of the portion or aspect of a personality that can observe and operate apart from its physical body. The operational tests of the existence of the soul consist in determining, by experiment or by rigorous observation of spontaneous cases, whether the focus of consciousness of given persons can actually bring back correct information about distant events not known through the senses, and whether that focus of consciousness can make its presence and its ideas and images known apart from the physical body. The evidence for the reality of the human soul, thus defined, has become so strong that the burden of proof lies upon those who deny its existence.

DOES THE SOUL SURVIVE BODILY DEATH?

We have said that the evidence points strongly to the reality of a soul that can observe and operate at a distance from the physical body. That is not the same thing as saying that the soul can observe and operate after its physical body has been destroyed. And it is this survival of bodily death that is the crucial question raised in the subject to which this lecture is addressed.

A moment ago we listed ways in which the soul has been reported to have made excursions away from the physical body — such as dreams, hypnotism and deliberate " mental " effort. But there is another type of departure of apparitions from their physical bodies — a type to which a great deal of systematic study has been devoted. This is the sort of case in which an apparition of a person is seen at the time, or very near to the time, when that person is dying.

A few minutes ago we mentioned the British scientists who questioned seventeen thousand people about apparitions. Of the 830 realistic apparitions reported, seventy-eight, or about one in eleven, were of people who died either exactly at the time when their apparitions were seen, or within twelve hours before or after. In seventy of these cases the persons who saw the apparitions had no normal knowledge that the persons represented by the apparitions were dead or that they were at the point of death. At the close of a searching study of these cases the investigators concluded:

We have shown that — after making the most ample allowance for all ascertainable sources of error — the number of these experiences remains far greater than the hypothesis of chance-coincidence will account for.[12]

These statistics become alive when we consider actual cases of the kind on which they are based. Let us review one such case, involving a dying mother who is reported to have left her body a few hours before her death, to pay her children a farewell visit. This case is over 250 years old, but it was so well investigated at the time that it may be taken as evidence that psychical research had begun to use scientific methods long before sixty years ago.

On June 4, 1691, Mrs. John Goffe died in her father's house in West Mulling, England. On the day before her death, Mrs. Goffe grew impatiently desirous to see her two children whom she had left at her own home, nine miles away, in charge of a nurse. Between one and two o'clock the next morning this dying woman fell into a trance, with eyes open and fixed, jaw fallen, and no perceptible respiration. Next morning she told her mother that she had been at home with her children during her sleep.

[12] *Society for Psychical Research Proceedings*, X (1894), 44, 208, 393.

The nurse who was watching the children said that she would " take her oath on't before a magistrate, and receive the sacrament upon it " that a little before two o'clock that morning she saw the likeness of Mrs. Goffe come out of the adjoining room, where the older of the two children was sleeping, and stand by the side of the bed where the younger child was sleeping with the nurse. The eyes and mouth of the apparition moved, but she said nothing. The nurse sat up in bed, spoke to the apparition, slipped on her clothes and followed it, but could not tell what became of it. She became so frightened that she walked up and down until she was able to rouse some neighbors at six o'clock, to whom she told her experience.

Within two days after the woman's funeral, Rev. Thomas Tilson investigated the case, and found that the statements of the various witnesses agreed in the same story, and that they appeared to be sober, intelligent persons.[13]

In the case just cited the mother, who was near death, reported having been nine miles away from her dying body. In several other cases an individual who seemed to be at the point of death — from heart failure, from an electric shock, from an operation or the like — has reported having seen from the outside his apparently dying body, but having regained consciousness within that body when it recovered.[14] These reports of experiencing an excursion from one's own body when death comes close are not in themselves evidential, but they fit beautifully into the general pattern. Taken with the excellent collections of evidence about apparitions seen at or near the time of death, they suggest the hypothesis that the bonds that unite soul and body are weakened as death approaches.

Apparitions of people who are dying give us a transition stage between conscious apparitions of the living and apparitions of

[13] Quoted from Richard Baxter's *The Certainty of the World of Spirits* in Robert Dale Owen's *Footfalls on the Boundary of Another World* (New York, c. 1870), pp. 187-189.

[14] See Nandor Fodor's *Encyclopædia of Psychic Science* (London, 1933), pp. 80-81, 104; *Society for Psychical Research Proceedings*, VIII (1892), 180-200; Sylvan Muldoon's *Projection of the Astral Body* (London, 1929), pp. 187-189.

persons known to be thoroughly dead. Let us now consider a fairly recent example of an apparition of the dead:

In an English village, in the year 1932, nine people at one time saw what appeared to be the living presence of a dead man closely related to them all. For a period of over a month, various groups from among these nine persons repeatedly saw this same apparition. The details are as follows.

In June, 1931, Samuel Bull died of cancer in Ramsbury, Wilts, England, leaving a grown grandson and a married daughter who, with her husband and five children, came to live with his widow. Eight months later, the married daughter states, she saw the deceased man ascend some stairs and pass through a door, which was shut, into the room in which he had died. Almost immediately afterwards the grown grandson saw the apparition. Later all the members of the family together saw it. Even the smallest girl, aged about five, exclaimed: " Why, there's Grandpa Bull." The appearances continued at frequent intervals from that time until April 9. Whenever the apparition was seen, all the persons present were able to see it. The apparition seemed solid, and twice laid his hand on the brow of his wife. Once she heard him call her name. On one occasion his figure was visible continuously for a period thought to have been a half-hour. He always appeared to be quite lifelike. The features were clearly recognized. He was dressed as he usually had been in the evenings when he had finished work. He was seen in daylight as well as by artificial light. The case was investigated by a distinguished committee within a month of the time when the apparition was last seen. The evidence was found to be consistent, and a signed statement testifying to the facts of the case was secured from two of the witnesses.[15]

This is only one of many cases in which apparitions of persons known to be dead have been seen by two or more persons at the same time. These collectively perceived apparitions, in turn, are but a small fraction of the total number of reported apparitions of the dead.

Notice now the way in which the evidence marches along.

[15] *Society for Psychical Research Journal*, XXVII (1932), 297-303. Used by permission.

First we note the conclusive proofs of telepathy and clairvoyance, based on more than 3,600,000 tests, which are summarized in *Extra-Sensory Perception after Sixty Years*. Next we try the experiment of imagining ourselves in the presence of some distant loved one; and we realize that if we and that loved one had full powers of telepathy and clairvoyance we might really see, touch and hear the distant one, while that loved one saw, heard and felt our apparition. We might thus commune together, even though our physical bodies were far apart. Then we note the fact that just such conscious apparitions of living people have been reported over and over again, from many different times and places. Next we find that a number of people have reported that, when their physical bodies neared death, their focus of consciousness moved outside, so that they observed their bodies from the exterior, as spectators. Next we note that apparitions of persons dying at a distance have been reported by people who had no normal knowledge of those deaths, and that these reports have come far oftener than students of the subject have been able to account for by chance. Finally we confront the fact that apparitions of the dead have also been reported, in all ages, by practically all peoples of whom we have adequate records, and that in many cases such apparitions have been seen by two or more people at the same time.

What conclusion arises from this series of facts? If we agree that the focus of consciousness of a living person can travel to a distance from his physical body, and can be seen as an apparition under circumstances that he later remembers, and if similar apparitions are seen of people whose bodies are dead — are we not driven to explore the hypothesis that these apparitions of the so-called dead may also be conscious, and may embody the focus of consciousness of the personality whose body has died?

But are the apparitions of the dead really similar in essential characteristics to the conscious apparitions of the living? A detailed study has been made of that question.[16] We lack the time here to review the evidence, but we can summarize the findings. First, apparitions of the dead almost always appear in ordinary clothing, not in ghostly winding sheets. So also do apparitions of the living appear in ordinary clothing. Second, apparitions of the dead usually adjust themselves to the physical surroundings in which they appear, as by passing through doorways, sitting in chairs, walking up stairways, looking at pictures on the wall, and the like. So also do apparitions of the living. Third, apparitions of the dead sometimes pass through physical matter, as by entering or leaving through a closed and locked door, or by passing through a solid wall. So also, at times, do conscious apparitions of the living pass through solid physical matter. Fourth, apparitions of the dead most often appear to people with whom they have strong emotional bonds, such as husband, wife or sweetheart, parent or child, close friend or bitter enemy. So too do conscious apparitions of the living. Fifth, apparitions of the dead tend to appear at moments of emotional crisis, danger, accident or shock. So too do conscious apparitions of the living. Sixth, apparitions of the dead are not only seen but sometimes heard to speak and sometimes felt to touch the one who perceives them. So also are apparitions of the living. In all six ways, therefore, the apparitions of the dead are found to be essentially the same sort of phenomena as are the conscious apparitions of the living. Since the two classes merge into each other, with no sharp line of demarkation, the most rational working hypothesis is that the apparitions of the dead, like those of the living, are, at least at times, the vehicles of the central focus of consciousness which says " I " within a personality. If this is true, then the conscious spirit does survive death.

[16] Hornell and Ella Hart, "Visions and Apparitions Collectively and Reciprocally Perceived," *Society for Psychical Research Proceedings*, XLI (1933), 246-249.

Precognition and Survival

Our exploration of the problem of survival has now brought us to one of the most baffling and perplexing aspects of psychical research. We have seen that telepathy and clairvoyance mean that consciousness transcends space. The self can, in some cases, escape from the physical body, and can observe at a distance what is happening and what other people are thinking. That fact is disturbing enough to our ordinary ideas of reality. But now we must confront a still more disturbing fact. Consciousness not only transcends space, but also transcends time. In some strange sense, the future is already in existence; and, on occasion, many different people have slipped over into that future and perceived events that later took place in detail in the physical world as they had been foreseen in vision.

One of the most widely read discussions of this problem has been set forth in the writings of an aviation engineer named J. W. Dunne. His first book, called *An Experiment with Time*, was published in 1927. In it he presented evidence that his own dreams dealt often with the future as well as with the past — not merely with the future as he imagined it, but with the actual future which was later to take place. He said that he believed this was true for everyone, and he suggested methods for testing the theory by means of recording one's own dreams. Various students have carried out his instructions, and have confirmed for themselves his general findings.

But Dunne's experiments were not the pioneer investigation in this field. In 1934 a British investigator, H. F. Saltmarsh, made a study of the hundreds of cases of apparent precognition that had been published through previous decades. He found 125 cases in which the insight into the future was announced either in writing or to other witnesses before the predicted event happened, and in which the fulfillment of the prophetic knowledge was confirmed by written documents or by independent witnesses. He concluded: " After prolonged study I have no hesitation in affirming that precognitions do occur." [17]

Saltmarsh reached his conclusion by a study of spontaneous cases. At the Duke University Parapsychology Laboratories and elsewhere various deliberate experiments in precognition have been carried out. For example, students have systematically recorded their guesses as to the order in which the cards would be found to lie when they had later been shuffled by machinery. Such experiments have confirmed the fact that flashes of knowledge of the future do occur. [18]

Here, then, is a proved fact. Real fragments of knowledge about the future do come into the minds of some people, erratically and even experimentally. What bearing does this fact have on our conclusions about survival beyond death?

To make our answer clearer let us imagine for a moment that our life here on earth is really a motion picture in three dimensions and in full colors. Let us suppose that our real selves are spectators, out in some dark auditorium. This great movie, called " Life on Earth," has its own time sequence. As we watch the play, let us suppose that each of us identifies himself or herself with some character, and begins to experience time as that character would experience it in the play. Now suppose that, by some error, part of one reel of the movie is shown ahead of its correct position; then this reel is put back into its proper place, and the play goes on. We should experience that misplaced scene " ahead of time," and when we came to it in its proper sequence it would be familiar to us, and we would have that odd feeling of knowing just what was going to happen next. That would correspond with our occasional recollection of precognitive dreams. But suppose that the next scene were to show the death of the character with whom we had identi-

[17] *Society for Psychical Research Proceedings*, XLII (1934), 63-71.

[18] For a bibliography on laboratory experiments in precognition see "An Experiment in Precognition Using Dice," by J. L. Woodruff and J. B. Rhine, *Journal of Parapsychology*, VI (1942), 262.

fied ourselves. We could still observe the subsequent scenes, if we chose, although our character would be out of the play. Or, if we preferred, we might get up and exit from the theater into a world that was not subject to the time sequences of the moving picture.

Some such view of reality seems to be forced upon us by the facts of precognition. Our physical personalities are mere vehicles, through which our real selves experience the drama called " life." Apparitions of the living are these same vehicles; through them consciousness may at times observe and operate apart from the physical body, and may temporarily depart from the play. But, if that view should prove to be true, then death in our physical world cannot extinguish the essential selfhood which says " I " in us. Apparitions of the dead are merely these same vehicles coming back into the space-time drama of the physical world from beyond. Our true existence is beyond both the space and the time of earth. And the event called " death " in our earthly lives can be but an episode in a far vaster adventure.

Fraudulent Mediums

The question of survival beyond death is of such passionate interest to so many people that there has grown up a great body of spiritualistic mediums and of occultists who offer, upon payment of money fees, to provide proofs of life beyond death, to put the bereaved into direct communication with the dead, to foretell the future, and to give advice and help from spirits about how to make money, cure sickness, succeed in love and acquire power. Many books have been written about the activities of commercial spirit mediums, some favorable, some unfavorable. But one outstanding conclusion of various studies by psychical researchers, and by professional sleight-of-hand magicians, needs to be recognized here. It is that a tremendous body of variegated fraud has grown up in this field. Some of the chief forms of fraud are as follows.

First we may note spirit photography. A wide variety of fraudulent methods have been exposed whereby alleged photographs of the spirits of the dead have been imposed upon the gullible. Careful students of this phase of spiritualism have reached the conclusion that no spirit photographs have been offered in evidence that might not have been produced by known fraudulent methods.[19]

Second comes slate-writing. Countless mediums have pretended to obtain messages from " the spirits," written on slates under conditions supposed to exclude human tampering. Hereward Carrington, a believer in the reality of many psychic phenomena, has pointed out more than fifty different methods of producing fraudulent slate-writing.[20]

A third type of fraud involves giving alleged spirit answers to questions written on paper that the medium pretends never to have seen, which he or she reads by one or another of a wide variety of sleight-of-hand tricks.

Fourth are séance phenomena, such as " spirit " rapping, table tipping, playing of musical instruments without apparent human contact, " levitation " of trumpets and other objects, making of " spirit " thumbprints in wax, alleged materialization of spirit forms and so on. These phenomena are usually performed in darkness, or with the aid of a curtained cabinet, or under other conditions conducive to fraud. According to one exposer of fake mediums, large commercial enterprises advertise that they will supply at stated prices apparatus to produce such phenomena by mechanical methods, and thou-

[19] See *Society for Psychical Research Proceedings*, XLI (1933), 121-133; John Mulholland, *Beware Familiar Spirits* (New York, 1938), pp. 147-157; Harry Price, *Fifty Years of Psychical Research* (New York, 1939), pp. 192-194.

[20] Hereward Carrington, *The Physical Phenomena of Spiritualism* (New York, 1920); Mulholland, *Beware Familiar Spirits*, pp. 109-121; Price, *Fifty Years of Psychical Research*, pp. 200-201. See also *Spirit Slate Writing and Kindred Phenomena*, by " Chung Ling Soo " (William Ellsworth Robinson) (New York, 1899).

sands of so-called spirit mediums are stated to have been found on their lists of customers. [21]

The foregoing areas of fraud do not by any means exhaust the list of such practices. But these four types of cheating have been so clearly proved that they may well stand as warnings. Whether or not the spirits of the surviving dead do ever produce physical effects in the sensori-motor world, such effects are very often fraudulently imitated by fake mediums who seek thus to get money from the credulous.

Wherever something precious exists, fraudulent imitations are likely to be offered. Counterfeit money, forged checks, imitation furs, fake diamonds, worthless mining stock, spurious works of art, hypocritical religion, pretended love, charlatan methods for healing disease — all these testify to the tendency to try to get money or power by offering false imitations of precious things. Sometimes a criminal offers something false when the real thing does not exist. Fake cures for cancer do not prove that real cures for cancer exist. But spurious mediumistic phenomena certainly do not disprove the existence of real mediumistic phenomena. Far oftener than not a counterfeit jewel exists because a real precious stone first existed to be imitated. Several very eminent scientists have testified that they obtained, under laboratory conditions, evidence to satisfy them that movement of objects without physical contact, and even the materialization of spirits, do at times occur.

The question of human immortality does not hinge upon the question of whether the physical phenomena of mediumship are ever genuine. We may therefore, at this point, present

[21] Mulholland, *Beware Familiar Spirits*, pp. 231-247; cf. G. N. M. Tyrrell, *Science and Psychical Phenomena* (London, 1938), p. 340; Price, *Fifty Years of Psychical Research*, pp. 208-212. It should be noted that, while Mulholland refers to "a number" of firms supplying equipment for fake mediums, he quotes from only one catalogue. Harry Price, in his subsequently published book, said that after a lifetime's search he had located only one such catalogue, whereupon he quotes from the same one cited by Mulholland, and reveals that it was published in 1901. This suggests that possibly these fraudulent firms may not be as numerous as Mulholland asserts.

three summary conclusions, and pass on. First, fraud is unquestionably widespread in the séances of professional mediums. Second, eminent and careful investigators have reported evidence that has convinced them that even the physical phenomena of spiritualism do sometimes genuinely occur. Third, satisfactory evidence of telepathy, clairvoyance, precognition and apparitions of the living and the dead have been obtained by so many careful investigators, at so many different times and places, that the most rational procedure is to adopt the existence of these as basic working hypotheses for further and deeper investigation.

COMMUNICATIONS FROM THE DEAD

One of the most frequent objections to belief in immortality is the scoffing question: "Well, if they survive death, why don't the dead ever tell us anything worth while?" In order to discuss this question intelligently it will be well to divide the alleged messages from the dead into four groups: first, those that seek to convince the bereaved of the survival of their lost loved ones; second, those that offer advice to the survivors about the conduct of their material affairs on earth; third, those that offer ethical and spiritual teachings; and fourth, those that purport to describe the nature of the life beyond death.

Examples of all four types are abundant. Each kind requires different tests as to its genuineness and value. Let us examine each briefly.

First, then, come the messages intended to identify the alleged survivor and to prove his or her continued existence beyond the grave. Mediums generally convey to sitters messages from alleged spirits who give intimate details to identify themselves — shared memories of small events, and facts such as only a close friend would know. Dr. John F. Thomas made a systematic study of such messages from twenty-two different mediums in Boston and in London. He took precautions to guard against their obtaining information by normal means. In the messages they gave him, 1720 points were made that could be checked up to determine whether they were true or false. Of these, more than 92 per cent were correct.[22] This average score of nine out of ten points correct is at least striking. The honest skeptic has a good deal to explain away when alleged communicating spirits, through twenty-two different mediums, without normal sources of information, make a score of 92 per cent correct out of 1720 verifiable points.

But a still more conclusive test was carried out at Duke University in 1935. Mrs. Eileen Garrett, taken into one room in the Parapsychology Laboratory, would go into a trance. A sitter unknown to her would then be taken into an adjoining room, with the door closed between them and a noisy electric fan running; neither the medium nor the sitter could see the other. A series of alleged messages from the dead would then be given for the sitter by the entranced medium, and these would be taken down by a stenographer without the sitter's hearing them. After twelve such sitters had had sittings, the transcripts of all twelve were given to each sitter; each was asked to indicate which of the statements in the messages seemed to be true as applied to himself, without any sitter's knowing which was the transcript taken when he himself was the person present in the adjoining room. Of course, some messages not intended for a sitter would seem to apply to him. But the overwhelming tendency was for each sitter to find the correct messages in the transcript that was actually taken when he was the sitter. The odds against the results' being due merely to chance are about 1,700,000 to 1.[23]

Not only information known to the sitter has been given correctly by mediums. Elaborate experiments have been car-

[22] John F. Thomas, *Beyond Normal Cognition* (Boston, 1937), pp. 128-148, 194-195. Cf. Tyrrell, *Science and Psychical Phenomena*, pp. 202-205.

[23] J. G. Pratt, *Toward a Method of Evaluating Mediumistic Material* (Boston, 1936).

ried out in which facts that have never been in the consciousness of the sitter have been correctly stated and have subsequently been verified. Long series of proxy sittings have even been held, in which the medium has given correct information in behalf of complete strangers, distant hundreds of miles from the sitting.

But, asks an objector, could not even these items of correct information come, not from the dead, but merely telepathically from the living or clairvoyantly from other sources? Yes, they could — if you ignore the rest of the evidence, and if you assume that the medium's extra-sensory powers are such that her mind can go out across the whole wide earth, through present and past lifetimes, and select from all the billions of people and places just the facts that can be fitted into a dramatic and lifelike message of identification, amazingly correct for the spirit who purports to be communicating. But remember that we are not offering these messages as our proofs of immortality. We have concluded that the focus of consciousness of a living person can sometimes observe and operate apart from his physical body. We have shown that this capacity would naturally result in the perception of apparitions of the living. We have shown that such apparitions are frequently observed. We have shown, moreover, that apparitions of the dying and the dead are of the same essential character as conscious apparitions of the living. And when skeptics object, " But if the dead survive, why do they never tell us anything worth while?" we answer, " They do tell us things that are worth while. The first kind of worth-while message they send consists in messages to prove their own identity. And these messages, in spite of varying percentages of error, are convincingly correct, with a correctness that cannot be due to fraud, coincidence or guessing."

The second kind of message from the dead consists of advice to survivors about the conduct of their affairs on earth. As an example of this group let us take the classical case of the Dutch

Ambassador's Lost Receipt, reported by Immanuel Kant in relation to Emanuel Swedenborg:

Madam Marteville, the widow of the Dutch Ambassador in Stockholm, some time after the death of her husband, was called upon by Croon, a goldsmith, to pay for a silver service which her husband had purchased from him. The widow was convinced that her late husband had been much too precise and orderly not to have paid this debt, yet she was unable to find the receipt. In her sorrow, and because the amount was considerable, she requested Mr. Swedenborg to call at her house. After apologizing for troubling him, she said that if, as all people said, he possessed the extraordinary gift of conversing with the souls of the departed, he would perhaps have the kindness to ask her husband how it was about the silver service. Swedenborg did not at all object to complying with her request. Three days afterwards the said lady had company at her house for coffee. Swedenborg called, and in his cool way informed her that he had conversed with her husband. The debt had been paid seven months before his decease, and the receipt was in a bureau in the room upstairs. The lady replied that the bureau had been quite cleared out, and that the receipt was not found among all the papers. Swedenborg said that her husband had described to him how, after pulling out the left-hand drawer, a board would appear, which required to be drawn out, when a secret compartment would be disclosed, containing his private Dutch correspondence, as well as the receipt. Upon hearing this description the whole company arose and accompanied the lady into the room upstairs. The bureau was opened; they did as they were directed; the compartment was found, of which no one had ever known before; and, to the great astonishment of all, the papers were discovered there, in accordance with his description.[24]

In spite of such examples, there are a number of good reasons for feeling that the search for spirit advice about our material affairs may easily become unwholesome. First, some observations I have made of spiritualistic gatherings in London, New York, Los Angeles and various other places have led me to feel that chronic seekers after spirit advice upon mundane matters

[24] Prince, *Noted Witnesses*, pp. 53-54.

are not generally well-balanced, healthy-minded, successful people. Second, in view of the established facts about mediumistic frauds, the person who accepts alleged spirit advice from the average professional medium is quite possibly substituting the fraudulent guesswork of a stranger for his own best judgment. Third, spiritualism very easily becomes an obsession, and throws a person out of adjustment with his normal life. Fourth, many spirit communications have stated that life on earth is intended to be a school of the spirit, where we are to learn through hardship and struggle. Just as a wise teacher does not solve most of the problems for his pupils, so wise spiritual guides cannot be expected to solve for us our earthly assignments of problems and difficulties. Fifth, there is a method of higher communion, called meditation, which, when truly and wisely used, and when combined with all the other available methods of seeking truth through reason, research and human advice, can lead us to a far sounder adjustment to reality than we can get by credulously following the real or alleged advice of disembodied spirits upon our workaday problems.

The third kind of message reported to come from the surviving dead consists of ethical and spiritual teachings. In regard to such communications, the crucial question is not as to the source but as to the living effect of the message upon one's life. I personally happen to have been greatly influenced and helped by such alleged spirit communications as Margaret Cameron's *The Seven Purposes*, and Stainton Moses' *Spirit Teachings*, and also by a good many books that purport to give accounts of the life after death. But, if facts of the sort set forth in this lecture are real, what we need is not so much individual revelations of a supernormal character, but rather a greater integration of our consciousness with spiritual reality, so that all our thinking and our understanding may be lifted to higher and higher levels. We need to cultivate the power of intuition by systematic meditation, and we need to test our intuitions by the most rigorous methods of science. In so far as our intellectual leaders ignore or repudiate the powers of the inner world, we shall be shut off from insights and illuminations that are vital to the growth of the human spirit.

The fourth kind of message consists of accounts of the life after death. Such accounts have come to us from very ancient times. Primitive peoples, not universally but very generally, have believed that the souls of the dead went on beyond the grave, in a life similar in many ways to their previous life on earth, but freed from most of the hardships and sufferings of earthly life. [25] Among ancient peoples this belief developed toward a recognition that the state of the soul after death depends upon the kind of character that has been built during life on earth.

In our modern times, we have been getting two kinds of reports from alleged observers of the life beyond the grave. One kind comes from communications allegedly received from the dead, through automatic writing, trance utterances and the like. The second kind come from various persons who tell of having made excursions outside of their physical bodies, of having explored the abodes of the dead, and of having brought back descriptions of what they observed. Some of the more interesting of these two types of modern accounts are listed at the end of this essay. These descriptions differ in many particulars, but the striking thing is the great amount of basic agreement they contain. Let me summarize very briefly some of the major points upon which the various accounts are fairly unanimous.

First, as to the experience of death itself. According to these reports, many people find, at death, that they are outside their physical bodies and are unable to get back into them. They can see their old surroundings and associates, but can no longer

---

[25] See passages indexed under "Future Life" in George P. Murdock's *Our Primitive Contemporaries* (New York, 1934). Cf. Boas, *Future Life*, pp. 24-25; and Lewis Paton's *Spiritism and the Cult of the Dead in Antiquity* (New York, 1921), pp. 8-9.

make themselves felt, seen or heard. Either just before death, or shortly after, they become aware of others who have died previously, whom they can see, touch and talk with. Some of the recently dead keep lingering around their old haunts on earth, still trying to experience their old bodily gratifications, and sometimes succeeding vicariously by taking partial possession of the living. Normally, however, the recently dead are led away by former loved ones or by ministering spirits into a new life, in which they are surrounded by visible and tangible objects — landscapes, buildings, furniture, books, tools, animals, plants and people. These things are recognizably similar to objects experienced on earth, and especially to surroundings experienced in vivid dreams. But they are different from earthly objects in important respects. Chiefly, one's surroundings after death are much more subject to being molded by one's thoughts, desires and purposes than are material objects on earth. One can travel by a mere act of will. One can create directly, by intense and persistent imagination, especially when the imagining is done collectively.

In this afterlife there are reported to be many regions, some happy, some unhappy. These regions differ widely in their dominant interests and activities. The individual after death tends to move, by spiritual gravitation, into regions where he associates with other people like himself, and where his surroundings are created jointly out of the collective memories, attitudes and aspirations of those with whom he is spiritually attuned. If he is filthy, cruel and treacherous, he moves into the sort of world that the subconscious and conscious minds of such people would create in their interactions with one another; and he must remain there until he is ready and willing to progress to better relationships. If one who dies is a lover of beauty, of truth and of his fellow men, he moves into the sort of world that such beings would create by the interactions of their personalities, and he goes on progressing from that state.

The sort of afterlife just described is repudiated, at first sight, by a considerable proportion of the more highly educated people who begin to inquire into such matters. They object to any conception of the life after death that seems to involve tangible objects, visible bodies which can act upon their surroundings, and activities that seem to be continuations of and developments from earthly occupations.

But let us go back to the fundamentals. If we should add a high degree of telepathy to the clearest and most rational of our dreams, we should obtain a world similar in essentials to the kind of afterlife just described. Rudyard Kipling's *Brushwood Boy* and George Du Maurier's *Peter Ibbetson* each offer the conception of lovers meeting in shared dreams. Various people have reported actual shared dreams, in which two or more persons have met each other, have observed their common surroundings, have conversed with each other, and later, after waking, have both remembered their shared adventure. If you ever become aware that you are dreaming, and if you are able to continue your dream with clear consciousness, try to apply these tests. Are not your surroundings vividly visible, in clear colors, with minute details? Are not the walls, the furniture, the ground and the objects around you tangible and solid? Do not at least some of the people you meet seem to be as real, as spontaneous and as original as the people whom you meet in your waking world? If, in your dreams, when your physical body lies unconscious in its bed, you move about in a dream body, very much alive, in a visible and tangible dream-world, is it so strange that those who bring us back accounts of a life beyond death should also tell us of tangible and visible objects and people in that afterlife?

It is true that in our dreams, as we usually remember them, we do absurd things, encounter jumbled memories from our waking life, and participate in scenes that psychiatrists can often prove to be symbolic representations of our repressed emotional tensions. It is true also that most mediumistic communications, even from honest mediums, and even when conveying genuinely evidential material, are likely to be jumbled, meandering and in some ways absurd. Mrs. Piper, one of the most thoroughly studied of all mediums, was purportedly controlled by a departed spirit who called himself Phinuit and who said he had been a Frenchman, but who knew no French, and who never gave any convincing proof of his existence as an independent spirit.

But, though most dreams seem to be confused, irrational and even imbecilic, many dreamers do at times have dreams that are marvelously clear, wise beyond all ordinary wisdom, and radiantly full of joy and inspiration. So, too, though many mediumistic utterances are rambling, there are numerous records of sittings in which the personalities of departed people have come back with convincing and dramatic vividness, giving clear evidence of their identity, and communicating teachings about the nature of the spiritual life that have lifted and transformed those to whom they were addressed.

A Spiritual View of Reality

What then are the conclusions to which this hour of shared thinking has brought us? We have confronted together one of the greatest problems of the ages. In our search for a working solution we have appealed to science. What is the answer that science gives?

Part of the answer is clear and explicit. The findings of research into the realms beyond the senses have destroyed the foundations of the rankly materialistic viewpoint which has flourished in our Machine Age. Many have been proclaiming in the name of science that personality is nothing but the physical body, with its sense organs, its muscles and its glands. Many have been proclaiming in the name of science that the only important reality is the material world, with its physical space, measured by steel surveyor's tape, and its time, measured by the swing of material planets and the tick of brass clock wheels. But now we are confronted with a science beyond the senses.

We see the accumulated results of laboratory experiments which tell us that the inner self can break out of the shell of the physical world and can perceive and act beyond the senses, defying space and time. The human soul is real. It can observe and operate apart from its physical body. Many scientists still deny these conclusions, but when they do so without refuting the accumulated evidence they violate the scientific method. The burden of proof has definitely shifted. The materialistic theory of existence is on the defensive. The spiritual view of reality is now the one that is supported by the weight of evidence.

Those who face these revolutionary facts are not necessarily compelled to believe in the immortality of the soul. Several keen thinkers have accepted telepathy but have repudiated belief in immortality. In order to maintain this disbelief, either they must construct elaborate hypotheses to explain away the facts of apparitions and of mediumistic messages, or else they must insist that the data are too scanty and uncertain to justify reaching any conclusions. To me the theories by which doubters have sought to escape from belief in immortality seem artificial and improbable. That is a question of judgment, upon which honest thinkers will differ. But to the honest agnostics who refuse to reach even tentative working theories I would say this:

Life here on earth is short. Our souls cry out for some working answer to the enigma of the ages. Better to explore courageously than to resign ourselves to doubt and confusion. Let us confront the probabilities of survival and of extinction. In the light of all available evidence, weighed as impartially as possible, let us adopt and act upon that working hypothesis that seems most simply and clearly to explain the known facts.

Here, then, are four conclusions by which we can go on living, with creative courage and with integrity, until scientific inquiries shall point the way to still sounder patterns of belief and of life:

First, this universe of ours is spiritual. Matter consists simply in the rigorous outworkings of the patterns by which Spirit acts and builds. We live and move and have our being within a Supreme Mind.

Second, our life here on earth is a drama, taking place within the Supreme Mind. Our immortal spirits are actors, cast in the roles of the divine comedy.

Third, death is merely our final exit in the character we have been playing in the present act. When we have said our last line we move into the wings, lay off our costume, wipe away the make-up and step through the stage door into a wider world. And sometimes, from realms beyond our theater of life, actors who have made the exit called death come back from the wider world and move for a moment among us, challenging our earth-bound personalities to look up and out beyond the stars. Far oftener, in our deepest hearts, we may hold communion with them.

Fourth, being privileged, for a little while, to move about upon the stage of Creative Life, let us explore reality reverently but courageously, knowing that our destiny reaches out far beyond the scenery, the make-up and the properties of this present stage of experience. Let us learn to tune our minds in with the Consciousness that is the Father of our spirits and the Author of our lives. Let us train and discipline our personalities, that we may fit ourselves to live more fully, now and forever, in the endless life of God.

Books Suggested for Further Study

General Books on Psychical Research

Hegy, Reginald. *Witness through the Centuries.* New York: E. P. Dutton and Co., 1935.

Myers, Frederick W. H. *Human Personality and Its Survival of Bodily Death.* Edited and abridged by Leopold H. Myers. New York: Longmans, Green and Company, 1913.

RHINE, J. B., STUART, C. E., PRATT, J. G., SMITH, B. M., and GREEN-WOOD, J. A. *Extra-Sensory Perception after Sixty Years.* New York: Henry Holt and Company, 1940.

TYRRELL, G. N. M. *Science and Psychical Phenomena.* London: Methuen and Co., 1938.

Some Studies of Precognition

DUNNE, J. W. *An Experiment with Time.* New York: The Macmillan Company, 1927.

SALTMARSH, H. F. " Report on Cases of Apparent Precognition." *Society for Psychical Research Proceedings,* XLII (1934), 49-103.

Some Studies Opposed to Spiritualism

BARNARD, G. C. *The Supernormal: A Critical Introduction to Psychic Science.* London: Rider and Co., 1933.

CAILLIET, EMILE. *Why We Oppose the Occult.* Philadelphia: University of Pennsylvania Press, 1932.

DODDS, E. R. "Why I Do Not Believe in Survival." *Society for Psychical Research Proceedings,* XLII (1934), 147-172.

HOUDINI, HARRY. *A Magician among the Spirits.* New York: Harper and Brothers, 1924.

JASTROW, JOSEPH. *Fact and Fable in Psychology.* Boston: Houghton Mifflin Company, 1900.

LAMONT, CORLISS. *The Illusion of Immortality.* New York: G. P. Putnam's Sons, 1935.

McCOMAS, HENRY C. *Ghosts I Have Talked With.* Baltimore: Williams and Wilkins, 1935.

MULHOLLAND, JOHN. *Beware Familiar Spirits.* New York: Charles Scribner's Sons, 1938.

PODMORE, FRANK. *The Newer Spiritualism.* London: T. Fisher Unwin, 1910.

Some Descriptions of Life beyond Death

FRANCHEZZO. *A Wanderer in Spirit Lands.* Transcribed by A. Farnese. Chicago: Progressive Thinker Publishing House, 1901.

LARSEN, CAROLINE D. *My Travels in the Spirit World.* Rutland, Vermont: The Tuttle Co., 1927.

OWEN, G. VALE. *The Life beyond the Veil.* London: Thornton Butterworth, Ltd., 1929.

THOMAS, CHARLES DRAYTON. *Life beyond Death with Evidence.* London: William Collins Sons and Co., 1930.

WARD, J. S. M. *Gone West.* Philadelphia: David McKay Company, 1920.

5

RELIGION AND MODERN KNOWLEDGE

Reinhold Niebuhr

REINHOLD NIEBUHR, professor of applied Christianity at Union Theological Seminary, is an ordained minister of the Evangelical and Reformed Church. Among his published books are *Leaves from the Notebook of a Tamed Cynic*, *Christianity and Power Politics* and *The Nature and Destiny of Man*. He is editor of the quarterly *Christianity and Society* and of the biweekly *Christianity and Crisis*.

5 *Reinhold Niebuhr*

RELIGION AND
MODERN KNOWLEDGE[1]

*J*T IS A FAIRLY simple matter to define the general character of " modern knowledge," about the influence of which upon religious faith we are to inquire. Modern knowledge is knowledge that has been influenced by the tremendous advance of natural science. Philosophical knowledge and speculation about the character of the universe have not greatly varied through the centuries. The problem between philosophy and religion has always been whether or not the principle of order and meaning given in the mind itself shall be equated with the religious idea of God. That is to say, the question has been whether rationality is identical with the religious sense of meaning, and whether the God whom religious faith apprehends behind and above the flux of passing things shall be defined as essentially the " logos," the principle of rational cohesion in the world.

The advance of modern science has shifted the debate. The question for moderns has usually been whether or not the principle of natural causation, as observed and as used by science, shall be regarded as an adequate principle of meaning for the world. In other words, is nature God? Causality has taken the place of rationality as the best principle of meaning in

[1] Delivered at Lancaster, Pennsylvania, as the Garvin Lecture for 1944, under the title, " The Idea of God as Affected by Modern Knowledge."

modern culture. In the older philosophy the idea of rationality was usually equivalent in some way with the idea of God. Therefore the ultimate question was whether man participated in the divine by virtue of his reason; or whether it was necessary to assume a more absolute mind, less touched by finiteness and contingency than the " logos " which came to expression in human life.

Since the rise of modern science the idea of natural causality has become the regnant principle of meaning. The order of nature has supplanted the order of mind as the symbol of meaning and order in the world. Preoccupation with the idea of " nature " has given us the modern ideas of a " natural law " which could be adduced from observing the facts of nature; of a " natural religion " which could be proved by pointing to the indubitable evidences of order and purpose in the world of nature; and of a " natural history " which would give meaning to the human enterprise by interpreting it in the light of its relation to nature.

Let us analyze this development in modern knowledge with reference to its effect upon the certainty of religious belief in God, and upon the quality of this religious faith. Such an inquiry may prepare us to redefine the problem of religious faith in its relation to any kind of knowledge, including modern knowledge.

I

Modern science has significantly prompted various scientists to make contradictory estimates of the relation of scientific knowledge to religious faith.

One group of scientists have come to the conclusion that a knowledge of nature and of natural causation must finally destroy any religious faith in God. They have come to this conclusion because they believe that, if you can explain all things in terms of natural causation and natural history, it is not necessary to have any further principle of explanation. You do not speak of the creation of the world by God, either as the Bible or as Plato conceived of such creation, if you can trace the course of evolution; for evolution explains every subsequent event by every previous natural cause.

It must be noted that this ostensibly very irreligious answer to the question of the source and end of life's meaning is also in a sense a most religious answer. It is irreligious in so far as it denies that the world as we know it needs any other explanation than the ordered sequences of nature. Therefore it challenges all older, and more rationalistic, mystical or Biblical-mythical efforts to find, or to define, a more ultimate and a more free source of what things are and an explanation of why they are what they are. It is religious, however, in so far as it regards " nature " or natural causation as, in effect, God. We must never forget the religious significance of ostensible irreligion. Our religion is always our expression of the meaning of life. No one lives without some sense of meaning and every universe of meaning has a " God " in it. The God of a universe of meaning is that which is not explained but by which things are explained. It is the final source of meaning. The God of modern naturalism is " nature." The final order of the world to which man must adjust himself, and the meaning of life which saves it from chaos, are given by " nature."

This kind of naturalism is usually defined as " materialistic," but it is more accurate to designate it as " mechanistic." It explains all things in terms of necessity. It assumes that every subsequent event follows necessarily from a previous cause. If it does not do this, if it recognizes that any event is only one of many possible consequences of a previous cause, the sequences of nature lose their final significance. In that case, either the world is a complete chaos of chance (an alternative that few people really hold because no one can live long either emotionally or practically in a chaotic world), or it must be assumed that there is a more ultimate cause and source of the givenness of things than the observable sequences of nature.

David Hume has taught us, incidentally, how erroneous it is to identify cause with sequence. Looking back over any sequence we are all inclined to become mechanists. The previous event always seems to be an adequate cause of a subsequent event. But if we look forward we know that this is not true. It only seems true after the event.

Natural causation is not an adequate final principle of meaning. It is usually held by scientists rather than philosophers, and particularly by scientists who have an implicit rather than a well-thought-out metaphysics. When the philosophers begin to meditate upon the relation between the order of nature and the total universe of meaning, they usually arrive at a more complex statement of the problem than the mechanists and therefore also at a more profound solution.

They are forced to look for a source of meaning deeper than mere natural causation in order to explain the emergence of novelty in the history of events. They therefore look for a dimension of reality that has more freedom in it than the mechanisms of nature. Secondly, they look at all the various sequences of nature, geological and biological, psychological and historical, and they find, or think they find, " teleological " or purposive elements in the relation of these various sequences to each other. This is to say that they take a more synoptic view of all the realms of reality and seek to know what holds all the realms together in some system of order. If these various realms are not held together, we do not have one world but many — which is to say that we do not have a world or a " universe " at all. There are of course all sorts of evidences of inclusive purpose in the world which we can find when we look for them. But it is important to observe that we could not find them if we did not presuppose them in our very search. Both the mechanist and the teleological naturalist and every other seeker for order in the world assume the faiths they seek to validate by their observations and analyses. This is a proof of the fact that the religious sense of meaning is always partly the presupposition and never purely the consequence of all scientific, philosophical and practical pursuits of men. Our effort to define just what meaning the world has always presupposes that it has meaning. Even the denial that it has meaning must presuppose some concept of meaning, from the standpoint of which it can be asserted that the world is meaningless.

The more reflective and philosophical reinterpretation of modern scientific knowledge therefore generally tends to produce a less overtly irreligious concept of meaning. On the whole, philosophy finds it difficult to accept mere nature as God.

The philosophical reinterpretation of modern scientific knowledge generally points beyond " nature " in the sense that it asks for some more adequate principle of meaning than natural necessity. Philosophy usually finds this where it has always found it — in the idea of " reason " or " rationality." Modern philosophy is well able to absorb the wealth of modern science; but it is significant that in doing so it proves " modern knowledge " to be less uniquely modern than is sometimes supposed. There are strong affinities between modern versions of idealism and the classical idealism of the Greeks.

" Reason " is philosophy's idea of God, because there is in reason, however conceived, a connotation of freedom, as well as of order. The God of reason may be an immanent God, working in the stuff of reality and giving it form. The idea that there must be a transcendently free source of power and form to account for the world may not be emphasized in philosophy, and usually is not. But there is always a greater appreciation of freedom, as against necessity, in philosophy.

That is why the God of philosophy is a more adequate principle of meaning for the world of man and history than is the God of science. (It must be observed parenthetically that we are identifying naturalism with science and idealism with philosophy only in the broadest sense. Not all scientists are naturalists and not all philosophers, certainly, are idealists. Yet

generally a reflective and explicit philosophy takes a more synoptic view of all realms of reality than is likely to be taken by
the implicit or covert metaphysics that usually accompanies
scientific speculations about the nature of reality.)

The God of philosophy is a principle of meaning that includes
man's world and human history, as well as the world in which
necessity rules, or seems to rule. If natural causality is the final
explanation of the world, everything in the human world that
transcends nature must be regarded as a mere epiphenomenon.
But the idea that reason is God not only does justice to the realm
of freedom which seems to lie beyond and behind the sequences
of nature; but also gives a better explanation of the relevance
between the order of mind and the order of nature, and helps us
to understand why, in the words of Leonardo da Vinci, the one
holds the key that unlocks the mystery of the other.

We arrive at the conclusion, therefore, that, while modern
scientific knowledge has tended to reduce the idea of God to
the concept of causality, it has not been able to displace the
older and more powerful philosophical concept of God as
"logos," as a principle of order and creativity that transcends
the mechanistic sequences of nature and explains the total order
of things more adequately.

It must be observed that, in the faith of the Hebraic and the
Christian tradition, God has been conceived of as a source and
end of life, who transcends both nature and reason. The idea
of a creator God — who is the source not only of the order but
also of the vitality of reality, who is both power and logos — as
it is held by classical religious faith, is more immediately irrational than the concepts of either science or philosophy. Causality and rationality are concepts of a source of order immanent
within the system of order. But in so far as they are immanent
they do not fully explain that depth of reality which seems to
lie behind and beyond any given system of order. Every
known system of order seems to point beyond itself to a more
ultimate source. If, for instance, we regard mind as God, we

must also assume, as Plato did, that the mind works upon some formless stuff to give it order. We must assume matter, in other words, to be as primordial as mind. But in that case we have a "universe" in which mind and matter are the two forms of givenness.

If we fully analyze this aspect of the universe and note all the loose ends that remain if we try to tie it together with any knot that we may be able to find within the stuff itself (whether the knot be the idea of causality or the idea of rationality), we must come to the conclusion that any principle within one comprehension is not adequate to give us comprehension of the whole, while any principle adequate for the comprehension of the whole transcends our comprehension. The irrationality of faith is the basis of rationality. The God of religious faith is the center and source of a meaningful world. The concept of God in science and philosophy may be the center and source of a rational order; but the order is too simple to include the totality of things in all their complexity. Rationality and meaningfulness are not identical. For classical religion the world is meaningful but not completely rational — though it is not denied that the order reason can discern is a part of the real meaning of the world.

In the sense that the faith of Biblical religion comprehends the totality of things more completely and adequately than any alternative faith, it may be regarded as rational. But, in the sense that God who is believed to be the source and end of all things transcends our rational comprehension, this faith is suprarational. This is a situation that will not be changed by the rise and fall of philosophical systems. It is a permanent situation. In so far as man has the transcendent freedom to survey his world, he must give a "rational" account of its order and coherence. In so far as he is himself involved in the finiteness of the world, he can only give this account by faith. Thus religious faith never stands in contradiction to reason but also can never be equated with it.

II

The second question to which we promised to address ourselves was in what way the advance of modern knowledge affected the quality of religious faith in God. Here it is necessary to give an answer that will shock the average " modern " mind, convinced as it is that all achievements of modern knowledge have added to the sum of human wisdom. The real fact is that modern culture's obsession with the realm of nature has falsified modern man's comprehension of ultimate reality. It has given him a thin and flat picture of the world.

Modern culture with its " natural religion " and " natural law " has not been very profound in its understanding of human history, or in its anticipation of the evils that might arise in history, or in its measurement of the heights and depths of the human spirit.

It has failed to understand the true height of the human spirit because it sought to comprehend man in terms of his relation to nature. Now man is quite obviously an animal, subject to nature's necessities and bound by its limitations and confined to the brief years which nature allows all her living forms. Man dies as animals die. But he knows that he dies, a knowledge that animals do not have. The knowledge by which he anticipates death is, in a sense, a proof that he is deathless, or at least that he transcends, by some capacity within himself, the flux of nature in which he stands. Man is a creature who transcends nature and finally himself. His history is grounded in nature but its pinnacles reach into eternity. This eternity is not infinity of time but the changeless principles that determine the changes of nature and history. Man is suspended between eternity and nature. That is why man can no more understand himself than he can understand the world without a principle of comprehension that transcends his comprehension. " That I might know him," declares St. Paul of God; "no, rather that I might be known of him." This expresses the final problem of religious faith very neatly. We seek to comprehend the world and God, but we know that the final problem is whether we are ourselves comprehended, whether there is a meaningful reality transcending the concepts of meaning that we have from our particular locus in the finite flux.

It is a great error to assume that modern knowledge has added to the dignity of man while classical religion has told us only of his misery. The fact is that neither the dignity nor the misery of man is fully understood in any philosophy that regards nature as God and that seeks to level man to the dimensions of nature. The dignity of man is his freedom, his capacity to make and remake history, to search out all things and to inquire after the meaning of existence. This dignity can be understood only in a dimension deeper and higher than what is generally known as " nature." Man is not just a slightly more clever animal. He is unique not only in the degree of his practical intelligence or in his inventive genius. His real uniqueness consists in the fact that he can make himself and the world the object of his thought and inquire into the relation of his self to the world.

It is true of course that in a classical Christian faith the misery of man is emphasized as well as his dignity. The eighteenth and nineteenth centuries falsely believed that if men would only live in the dimension of nature they would be harmless. The philosophers of the modern period believe that human selfishness would be harmless if only governments did not interfere with human behavior. The reason they had this illusion was that they thought " nature " set natural limits to human egotism. But the real fact is that human ambitions and desires are boundless. Thus the dignity and the misery of man spring from the same source — from his freedom. Man is a creator because he is not absolutely bound by nature. Man is also a sinner because he is not so bound. The animals know no community but that of the family and herd. Man builds larger and larger communities and constantly extends the breadth and extent of the moral obligation men feel for each other. But the same man also allows these communities to conceive boundless imperial ambitions. And the same science that holds vast communities together by modern means of communication also makes conflicts between these communities deadly beyond any parallel known in nature. "The superman built the airplane and the ape man got ahold of it," declared a modern scientist in explaining our modern predicament. This is true only if it is understood that the superman and the ape man are the same man, and that the evil described by the term "ape" is wrongly described. For the evil of human history is not the vestigial remnant of the ape in man; it is the boundless character of human ambitions and the limitless character of human self-love, particularly collective self-love and pride.

Man is a creature who is neither bound by the necessities of nature nor yet completely disciplined by the cool calculations of reason. He can use both nature and reason to serve his purposes.

There are forms of modern knowledge, such as psychiatry, that have illumined the dark and cavernous recesses of the human ego below the level of reason, though they have usually wrongly defined this subrational cellar of the human psyche as purely biological. There are also forms of modern social knowledge that have traced the whole sad story of man's inhumanity to man. But no characteristically modern form of knowledge has done full justice to the majesty and tragedy of human existence. No *Divine Comedy* or *Don Quixote* has come out of our modern culture, nor has it produced anything like Dostoevski's *Crime and Punishment*.

The reason for this lack is that the human drama has not been measured in its true dimension. It has been regarded as merely a little final chapter in the story of natural evolution. Or it has been thought of as a simple story of the growing rationality of man. But, if by "reasonable" we mean the capacity to confine the human spirit and the human aspirations into some simple measure of prudence, man is not, and will never be, rational.

We have not understood man or his history in the modern period because we had too simple a religion. We thought of the religions of old as credulous; but the credulity of the modern man exceeds all forms of ancient credulity. Modern culture thinks it easy to bring two racial groups into a harmonious relation to each other. This is, in fact, very difficult, because each group has its own pride and arrogance, corruptions of its justified will to live. Modern culture thinks it easy to form a government of the world. But this final and necessary task in man's community building is desperately difficult, and we may not succeed in it until we have undergone the chastisement of war many more times. The reason is that it is difficult to bring the pride and self-will of nations, particularly great nations, under the dominion of a greater sovereignty. Human history represents limitless possibilities of good, but also of evil. The good that is possible in human history is finer than the calculated forms of prudence that go by the name of virtue in modern culture. The evil in it is something more than the inertial force of " nature " or ignorance, holding back against an advancing mind. The evil represents a positive threat to order, derived from man's spiritual capacities, from the boundless character of his ambitions and desires.

Thus the picture of life that we have in modern culture is untrue because its picture of God is not true. Its universe is too flat. Its principle of meaning is too simple. It does not understand that only a God who has the power finally to beat down all human rebellions against his majesty, and the mercy to draw the evil of history into himself, can really be the God and sovereign of this sad and majestic human enterprise.

III

If we seek for a more adequate idea of God today, our search must be informed by a full understanding of the inadequacy of any concepts of coherence and order drawn merely from the observation of nature. It is in fact the tragedy of our age that the great advance of natural science should have determined our ultimate religious and philosophical ideas, while at the same time human history became the scene of titanic struggles which made it crystal clear that man's life is not confined by natural limitations, that nature's harmonies do not set limits to his ambitions either for good or for evil, that nature's serenity is not redemptive for man because it knows nothing of the disquiet of his spirit and that nature's dimensions do not fulfill his life. Put in other words, an adequate religion must do justice to the meaning of human history and not annul it.

This means that it must do justice both to the freedom of man in history and to the evil which is made possible by that freedom. It must, in the words of Pascal, understand both the dignity and the misery of man. It must be able to apprehend a depth of reality in which the dignity of man has meaning and in which the misery of man is finally overcome.

When one explores the ultimate issues of life one rediscovers the relevance of the Biblical faith in God as against the modern substitutes given to us by the influence of so-called modern knowledge. I think it important to reassert the profundity of that Biblical faith in contrast to the tendency of past decades, in which the effort was made to reduce the meaning of Biblical faith until it would conform to the certainties of modern knowledge and the prejudices of modern culture.

Let us consider first the relation of the Biblical God to the freedom of man. According to the faith of the Bible, God is the creator of the world and the sovereign of human history, under whose providence the tortuous and tragic processes of history develop and are finally transmuted into redemptive possibilities. This means that man is not bound by either the virtues or the necessities of nature in a final form. "All things are yours . . . and ye are Christ's; and Christ is God's," declares St. Paul. This is to say that the final norm of our freedom is the norm of God, and not either nature or mind. Nature may reveal itself in us primarily as the survival impulse, but that does not mean, as the eighteenth century believed, that the impulse to survive is normative for us. Nature may have some forces of community in it, some forms of mutual aid, as P. A. Kropotkin and others have averred. Nature's communities are, however, very limited, being confined to family and herd, which is to say, to those forms of togetherness in which life is related to life by natural instinct. But man knows no limit to the obligation to conserve the life of his fellows. Thus history drives him to build larger and larger communities and he knows that finally his spiritual life stands under the warning of Jesus: " If ye love them which love you, what thank have ye?"

The freedom of man expresses itself not only in the indeterminate possibilities of community but in his final transcendence over all social and communal life. Man must fulfill himself in community but he cannot fulfill himself completely in community. Even the most perfect community is frustration as well as fulfillment for the human spirit, if for no other reason than that man is able to recognize the finite and temporal character of every social process. He dies, and his nations and empires also die; yet man is able to transcend this process of life and death and ask what meaning it has or whether it has meaning.

In answering that question he may, as in philosophical faith, come to the conclusion that the God who presides over this process is the reason that is evident in the world and in man himself. He may find peace in the idea of the immortality of the rational part of himself, conceived as part of the divine principle of life. But man's reason is also touched by finiteness; and it is in any event organically related to his body, more completely related to it than the immortality doctrines of the rationalists appreciate.

There is no meaning in this whole historical process at all if it is not held together by a higher sovereignty and governed by a stronger power than any force to be detected in either the nature below man or the mind within man. This is why the

Biblical faith in a sovereign God, beyond our comprehension, but without whom we are unable to comprehend our life, is the only adequate faith for understanding life in its full dimension.

But the dignity of man is only one of the two facts of human history that have not been fully comprehended in modern culture. The other is the misery of man. Man's freedom has been underestimated, but so has the evil he does in that freedom. Man's history is majestic but also incredibly tragic. Little in human history corresponds to the conception of a tame and prudential person which was the eighteenth century's ideal of man. The history of man is filled with creative achievement and with tragic corruption. Empires, nations and cultures rise, but also fall. And when they fall, they do so not by some necessity of nature but because they make some mistake in the realms of " spirit." Ruling classes cannot limit their pride or lust for power. Great nations become the cause of their own destruction by aspiring to a height and majesty to which no human and finite achievement has a right. Outmoded forms of communal organization are defended hysterically against new necessities of brotherhood, not by ignorance but by a kind of proud stubbornness. Every racial and economic group, every cultural and religious group, generates a pride which makes community with other groups difficult. We call this racial and religious prejudice; and we usually attribute it to a vestigial remnant of tribal parochialism. But the disease of race pride has a more positive note in it than mere ignorance, and is more difficult to eradicate than is usually assumed.

Thus human history is filled with the monstrous evils of man's inhumanity to man, raised in our own day to the tragic proportions of a world-wide tyranny, requiring a world-wide war for its defeat; and creating new perils and possibilities of evil in the very process of defeating the evil. These facts are so obvious that no one can deny them, though for some decades we sought to obscure their significance by interpreting these large-scale conflicts as momentary aberrations in a general pattern of progress. The Christian answer to the problem of man's misery — the faith in a just but also merciful God, who finally destroyed the evil of man in his own body, by taking the sin of man upon and into himself — was regarded as completely irrelevant to modern men, because we had a simpler and easier faith in redemption.

We believed that history itself was redemptive. We believed that the evolutionary process in nature was a guarantee of human progress in history. We thought that the course of development from amoeba to mammal and from mammal to man also guaranteed that a bad man would finally become good. There is of course no evidence for this curious faith. The highest forms of evil can be achieved only by the highest instrumentalities of civilization. Nazi corruption can arise only against the background of a highly integrated civilization; and it is effective only as it uses the instruments of that civilization for its destructive purposes. The idea that history is redemptive is a curious illusion arising from the fact that history is creative. It is indeed creative and develops higher and higher potencies. But as long as man has freedom he can misuse those potencies. There is no guarantee in either a rational or a natural process that man's capacity for evil can be destroyed. If this were the case his capacity of freedom would also be destroyed. His goodness would become merely the fruit of some natural or rational necessity. There would be no virtue in it.

If there is any meaning in human history, therefore, this can be the case only if it stands under the sovereignty of a God who does not destroy human freedom. But this means that the final ground and end of human existence not only must have the resource to beat down the rebellion of man's pride against the laws of creation (that is, the justice of God); but also must have the final resource to overcome the sin of man in history by his mercy.

The Biblical conception of the divine sovereign is that of a just and merciful God; of a God whose final majesty and power is revealed in the power of his mercy, which both negates and fulfills his justice. For Christian faith the Cross of Christ is the symbol of this ultimate mystery of the divine, never fully comprehended by human reason and yet not fully mysterious to human faith. This is the divine ground in which human history has its end and its fulfillment. Here is where the partial meanings of human history are completed. Here is where the contradictions of human history to the will of God are finally overcome without either destroying the freedom of man or negating the significance of the conflict between good and evil in history.

The Biblical conception of the divine is not that of an undifferentiated eternity in which all history, including the distinction between good and evil, is swallowed up. Nor is it that of an endless time, an infinity of time, in which the distinctions between man and God, history and eternity, are gradually narrowed and disappear. It is the conception of a divine sovereign who has created man in freedom and finitude; who alone can complete the human enterprise, because man is too finite to do so; but who can complete the historical adventure only by love and justice, because all other methods would destroy the creative responsibility of man.

Faith in such a God is a more adequate principle of interpretation and of action than the simpler and more obvious interpretations. This faith is foolishness until it becomes clear that all lesser faiths leave large sections of human experience and history in chaos; and that there is always a large realm of chaos of evil in human history over which there is no immediate, but only an ultimate, triumph of meaning. In this sense the foolishness of Christian faith can become the wisdom of God.

It can also become the power of God, because by this wisdom it is possible to be active in history, to accept responsibility in it without the alternate moods of illusion and despair that characterize modern culture. By such a faith we can wage war against extravagant forms of evil without nerving ourselves with the illusory hope that the victorious end of the war will also bring a victory of all righteousness. These illusions produce despair when it becomes known, as it must, that history remains ambiguous even after the victory of the best cause. We can work for a better world order, a more stable peace and more just relations among the nations, without the illusion that it is possible to create a perfectly safe and perpetual peace. This hope is also an illusion because nothing is absolutely safe in history. The illusion produces despair because the insecurity of history always reveals itself in the end — if not in our generation, then in the generation of our children. Man has no final security except in the sovereignty and majesty of God who presides over history and can make man's wrath to praise him. If we know that, we will not seek false securities in the insecurities of history.

In such a faith we can live bravely with a certain attitude of nonchalance toward the world's changing fortunes, always persuaded that " whether we live, we live unto the Lord; and whether we die, we die unto the Lord: whether we live therefore, or die, we are the Lord's."

6

IMMORTALITY IN THE LIGHT OF SCIENCE AND PHILOSOPHY

William Ernest Hocking

WILLIAM ERNEST HOCKING, Alford professor of philosophy (Harvard) emeritus, has also taught at Yale University, Andover Theological Seminary, and the Universities of California, Glasgow and Leiden. *Types of Philosophy, Thoughts on Death and Life* and *Science and the Idea of God* are among his published works.

6 *William Ernest Hocking*

IMMORTALITY IN THE LIGHT OF SCIENCE AND PHILOSOPHY[1]

*I*F THERE IS any such person as "the modern man," he is not one who worries much about the question whether human life continues beyond death.

For some, there is no worry because the question is closed, either for or against immortality. I have met a few human beings, not many, who profess that they have never doubted that life goes on in another world. They are not unintelligent people; they are fully conscious that they are in a minority. I regard their assurance as important, if only because it shows that such a conviction is wholly consistent with a modern mentality.

I have met others, indeed many more than in the first group, for whom the question is closed because they have completely rejected the belief, and have no inclination to reopen the problem. They do this usually on scientific grounds; and it is usually an acquired position — that is, it results from abandoning an earlier acceptance or at least entertainment of the hypothesis of immortality. We are certainly not born with the scientific conception of the universe. But when that view dawns on us, with its full clarity and unity — the persuasive alliance of human with animal life in the evolutionary series — it is likely to

---

[1] Delivered at Lancaster, Pennsylvania, as the Garvin Lecture for 1945, under the title, "The Immortality of Man."

melt away all beliefs that appear inconsistent with it. I can speak from my own experience in saying that immortality is one of these apparently inconsistent beliefs. As a boy I read Herbert Spencer, and was fully persuaded by him that man can have no other destiny than that of the animal series from which he comes; that in both cases the birth, growth, decline and death of the body are paralleled in the history of the mind. Without a brain, there can be no thoughts; and, when the brain dies, thought ceases. This, of course, is not a proof; it is only an analogy. But the analogy is so complete that it throws the burden of proof strongly on anyone who questions it. Hence, for many today, the question no longer exists.

But if I can estimate the position of the majority of our compatriots today, they have ceased to concern themselves about the problem of immortality not because it is settled but because it is, as they say, speculative. And they have been led to believe, first, that we cannot *do* anything about it in any case: it will either happen to us, or not happen, as the universe provides. If it does, we may be agreeably surprised; if it does not, we shall never know of our disappointment; the only thing we can really affect is the present scene of things — let us deal well with this. They have also been led to believe that we cannot *know* anything about it: we can only conjecture. And, where there can be no evidence, valid either in the court of science or in the court of law, wise men will refrain from judgment.

I regard it as one of the signs of the shallowness of our age that this indolent and defeatist point of view is so prevalent. As long as there are some good and intelligent people who regard immortality as unquestionable and, for them, certain and important, it is pure laxity of mind to retreat from the search for evidence. And, if it should be discovered that immortality is either actual or possible, it is again an attitude of moral abandonment to decide without inquiry that nothing can be done about it. Millions of people have believed and do now believe that everything we do in this life has an inescapable effect in a life to come. Many have believed and continue to believe that this life is a sort of preparation for another life, and has its chief meaning in that relationship. Some have believed and do believe that the manner of our living here may determine the question whether we do or do not survive the crisis of death — my own view.

If any of these people are right, there is a great deal to be done in the present about a future life.

This present idleness of mind on this great subject — out of which I should like to shake this generation if I could — is in extreme contrast to the preoccupation of a few generations ago with the future fate of their souls. To them the whole point of religion lay in the issue between future torment and future bliss. The imagination was so busied with this enormous gamut of hope and fear as to subtract a good deal from the attention due to present business. Karl Marx was not entirely wrong when he described this kind of religious concern as an opiate, fixing men's minds on the subjective condition of their consciences and withdrawing their energies from the social struggles in which objective rights and wrongs were contending. Through the obvious justice of such criticisms as these, religion has — for the most part — swung far in the other direction. Without surrendering its central doctrine that there is an infinitely important difference between being " saved " and being " lost," it has been inclined to teach that nothing very bad will happen in a future life to a man who fights the good fight here, and that nothing very good will happen to a man, however pious, who neglects that present duty and conflict. The great thing, then, for both worlds is to be a good citizen of this one. From this plausible position, it is but a short distance to the position that the whole duty of man is to watch the step just ahead of him, and leave the rest to God.

Professor Julian Huxley, the British biologist, recently wrote as follows: " The only rational attitude to take, until conclusive evidence of the fact of survival is forthcoming, is to concentrate on the enrichment and amelioration of this life, in confidence that if our personalities do survive death, a sane and hopeful activity in this world is the best preparation for the next." This is also the position of the religious humanism of today.

The difficulty with this position is that, in order to fight well as a man, one must fight as if one could reasonably disregard danger and even death; and to do this one must believe that there are things in the world more valuable and more enduring than human life itself.

To put this idea into a nutshell: It is impossible, I maintain, to make a reasonable contrast between being a good citizen of this world and having a concern for immortality, because in order to be a good citizen of this world, whether to do a good job or to fight a good fight here, one must have an outlook beyond this world.

HAS THE BELIEF IN IMMORTALITY ANY PRACTICAL EFFECT?

Here I think I hear a chorus of objectors. It will be pointed out that the good work and the good fighting done in this present war appear to be wholly independent of whether a man does or does not believe in immortality. It is enough to mention the armies of Soviet Russia which are officially materialist in outlook, so far as they take the party line. There is no difficulty in getting up suicide squads in any of the contending armies, regardless of the presence or absence of the hope of a future.

I agree to all this, and yet I hold to what I have said. The immediate inspiration of men lies in the *cause* for which they are working or fighting. It belongs to the ordinary sociability of the human being to be welded together strongly with his fellows whenever there is a cause — especially if the cause is under fire — that evokes common efforts and sacrifices. Working for the cause heightens fellowship; fellowship in turn heightens the devotion to the cause. Nobody reaches the summit of his capacity as a man until he has felt the experience of being lifted above himself by the power of this threefold relationship: the self, the fellow man, the common cause. Friendship itself is comparatively empty unless it is enlarged by the presence of this comparatively impersonal third being, the object that both friends serve and both obey.

The cause need not be from our point of view a good cause in order to produce this effect upon those who serve it. Any national cause is likely to elicit this kind of devotion; all kinds of isms, including fascism, Nipponism and Nazism, have had their enthusiastic or fanatical adherents. It is only necessary that these adherents believe in that cause, whether through indoctrination or illusion or through some glimpse of truth under grotesque disguises. To say that they must believe in the cause is to say that they must think of it as something better than their private point of view, their *parti pris,* that which seems to them to be good because they are born that way: they must fancy themselves as getting hold of something genuinely valid and just.

And now let us take another step. Those who *truly* believe that their cause is valid and just, and those who *mistakenly* believe that their cause is valid and just, have something important in common, as against those who do not care whether their cause is valid and just or not. These first two groups believe that there is something valid and just in the universe. This belief links them with something not perishable, which is the first stage in an outlook beyond this world.

And if they were to think this out — which most of them do not — they would find themselves inquiring into personal immortality. They would begin to realize that this idea was assuming for them an immense practical importance. Let me indicate briefly why this is the case.

The reason that a cause is or may be more important than a human life is that a good cause, like just government, will continue to knit together countless human lives throughout human history, once it is achieved, or to the degree in which it is achieved. Justice is sometimes said to be a " value ": that is, as an idea, it is something that rational beings recognize as a standard to be appreciated, worked for, embodied in institutions. As a logical idea, it belongs to the category of " values "; but as a working factor in the real world it is a value only if and when it is valued, when some mind takes it as a cause to be served. Destroy the minds, and justice vanishes into the status of an ineffective definition.

Hence it is that all those who serve causes assume that there will always be minds to care for them: they take for granted the continuance of the race, and the identity of the ideas the race cherishes. But suppose that some cosmic catastrophe wipes the human race out. Suppose that the planet freezes, and the last man sinks into an icy sleep. That assumed perpetuity is gone. Now nothing is valuable in fact, for there are no minds to value anything. In a dead universe nothing has any worth at all. Hitherto the death of the individual has been, in some degree, compensated by the continuance of the species. Now the species fails, and can anything compensate for *its* death?

The answer has to be, " Nothing," unless the individual, who appeared to die, does in fact continue to live. It is the individual in the last resort that must make up for the mortality of the race, not the race for the mortality of the individual.

Nature, it has been said, cares for the species and sacrifices the individual. It lavishes its care on the resources of reproduction; it exhausts the energy of the parent in the launching of the child, but only because the child in turn will be exhausted for the sake of *its* child. When that is done, the hollowed shell lives on as a wraith that men may cherish but nature merely tolerates. But this picture attributes to nature too great solicitude, even for the race. In point of literal fact, nature cares for nothing; for it has no care, it has only necessity. Nor does the race care for itself, for the race has no separate consciousness. The only thing that can care is an individual.

If, then, the race is cared for, it is because individuals care for it. And if in the end those things that the race builds up in works of technical power, in works of art, in products of thought and of the ethical prowess seen in systems of law and trade — if these things have any value in the universe, it is because individual egos somewhere appreciate them.

Then what men mean when they sacrifice themselves for a cause, whether they are aware of it or not, is that the valuers of the world must somehow last. The meaning of their sacrifice lies in the tacitly assumed endurance of the human soul.[2]

And here lies the practical value of the belief in immortality: though men do not know that their devotion to causes assumes that belief, when it is renounced the scheme of human values slowly becomes sick, as of a mysterious anemia. Nothing can have full dignity that has only transitory being. When all that men serve is taken as passing, life can continue its gaiety, its fervor, its energetic resolve, its constructive passion and its angers that strive to the death — but all of this has to be referred to the pattern of vital drives, because it can no longer be referred to a defensible reason. The irrational becomes the accepted excuse for human action; and activity is taken as a merit for its own sake, because no other merit can be found. A civilization that has embraced the causal scene of nature as its largest scheme of truth does not cease to operate; that is precisely what it continues: *operation* — the viscera generate their energies, the limbs continue to swing, the gusto of pleasure increases — for it must fill a void, and the bravura of achievement stirs a growing pride. For what the universe cannot applaud must wait for the *banzais* of the crowd. Nothing changes but the quietly

---

[2] And, once this is seen, the folly of that biological judgment becomes obvious. The individual, in his reproductive capacity, throws off a new generation as his pledge to the future. In so doing, instead of exhausting himself as an individual he matures himself; for he assumes a mental as well as a physical responsibility for the ongoing human stream, so long as it may endure. He does this from his superabundance; and having done it he remains himself, more completely than before. He has shown that the race is contained in him, the individual.

growing emptiness at the center, and the fear of rational analysis carried to the bitter end. Man can no longer face the question, *Cui bono?* — for he knows that he has in advance made the answer impossible.

The other day I met a man who had found out what his life had to mean to him. He was a manufacturer, and a successful one in the business way. He was even more successful as a reader of the distracting scene of the present human anguish. Men must suffer, he said, in order to learn; there are terrible lessons for our group life and for our personal life, and we shall not learn them in ease; we reject the effort to learn until terror and blood consume our best. The race is trying to unlearn its greed and its grasping for power; the exploiters have to unlearn the will to exploit, and the exploited have to unlearn their own ignorance and sloth and envy and the will to depend on public charity and the gangster arm of the labor patriot. All have to unlearn the materialism of the flesh and the sluggishness of the spirit. But why must we learn these things? For it is just the learning that is difficult; the immensest lethargy is the lethargy of the spirit which so slowly heaves itself into the atmosphere of love. Why must we learn?

Here his answer was simple, direct and unhesitating: we must continue to live. The meaning of the world is the development of the personal soul, a task unfinished in any one life. It is God's plan for us that we learn and forever continue to learn.

With this clue, he could take what came to him; he could learn the art of learning from those who unjustly opposed him — by finding what William Butler Yeats called the " pilgrim soul " in them also. And he could hold a steady head in full view of the slaughter of men and nations in the vast catastrophe of war. For to him the ultimate evil was not death, but the hardening of the mind against truth.

I do not say that his solution is the true one; I certainly do not say that it is final. But I say that an outlook like his, which fills his life with zest, leaves him resilient against immense losses, makes him a source of strength to many other men, is of immense practical importance. So far from being disaffected from active life, he has something from which the sagging morale of this era might be rejuvenated — provided only that it were true.

But can it be true?

Here, I turn to address myself to those for whom the problem of immortality is an open question, and who feel it important enough to worry about. They feel the force of the scientific position — that is to say, the usual attitude of scientific men. But they are ready to believe that this attitude may be mistaken, provided there is any substantial ground on which an affirmation of continuance could be built. They are unwilling to resort to a will to believe; they fear, rather than court, the influence of their own wishes. Just because the continuance of personal life would be so desirable to them, and so vastly important if it were true, they resist any direct appeal to their desires as evidence of fact. On this point, perhaps more than on any other, they are resolved not to delude themselves by wishful thinking.

I very much respect this state of mind; I would even urge those for whom the matter is already settled to adopt it hypothetically, for the sake of the argument ahead of us.

I propose that we take up first certain objections to the belief in immortality from the side of science and of philosophy, because in dealing with them we shall see more clearly what positive grounds for the belief there could be.

THE SCIENTIFIC OBJECTION

Let me first make clear that science does not deny the possibility of immortality. The field of science is this world of nature; it knows nothing of any other world. The term " world " in this sense includes, of course, the entire universe within the single space-time continuum which is the field of our gravitational-electrical relationships. Whatever belongs to this causal system belongs to nature in this sense.

I say that science does not deny the possibility of another universe, or of other universes. It does, however, doubt whether the suggestion that there might be other such worlds has any assignable meaning. It calls to witness here certain newer developments of logic or of semantics concerned with the meaning of " meaning," and interested in saving mankind fruitless speculative worry by marking off the realm of inquiries that have significance from those that have none. The general trend of opinion among semanticists is that metaphysical statements — among which we must include any statement about another life — are either meaningless, or else devoid of *scientific* meaning, though they may still have a vestige of emotional meaning.

On the basis of this doubt, science today is disposed to ignore the question of immortality as in any case beyond its jurisdiction. To our question it answers neither " no " nor " yes." But it tends to make the proposal of survival appear increasingly improbable, and on one specific ground — that of the precise fitness between mind and body. Mind and body vary together at every point. Aristotle has the distinction of first drawing attention to the force of this fitness, as a refutation of the fancies of Plato that the soul might not only leave the body and wander through the realms of Hades, but also return in another body differently disposed and equipped. For Plato adopted the belief in transmigration, as well as the belief in immortality; and he thought the mind might be better off without any body at all, so far as clear vision of truth is concerned.

Aristotle very rightly observed that the mind of one man would not fit the body of another: the mind of Homer could not be transferred to the body of Solon; still less could the mind of man take up its abode in the body of a tiger, or that of a tiger in the body of a man. Transmigration, then, was an absurdity; and, as Aristotle felt, the idea of a soul without any body at all was still more absurd, since what we mean by the soul is nothing more or less than the inner life of a given body, its guide in growth and behavior; in Aristotle's somewhat difficult phrase, the soul is the " form " of the body, and therefore not conceivable apart from the body requiring that particular form. Aristotle would have relished the problem dealt with in a seventeenth-century Harvard thesis — whether the speech of Balaam's ass required a temporary alteration of the animal's vocal cords!

Now this observation has been rather enforced than weakened by all the subsequent growth of our knowledge about the relation between mind and body. We have learned to associate the mental life, not with the body as a whole, but more directly with the brain and the central nervous system. And, while most thoughtful men recognize that the mind is not the same thing as the brain, or as the physiological action of the brain, they will agree that the activities of the mind and of the brain go along so closely together as to imply an exact mathematical relationship. Just what the relation is still eludes analysis; but much hope is placed on recent inquiries which indicate that there are electrical phenomena accompanying mental action from whose shape it is possible to infer, not one's thoughts, to be sure, but the gross distinctions between sleeping and waking, effort and rest, anxiety and peace. We know infinitely more than Aristotle of the extremely sensitive response of the mental condition to variations in the chemical constitution of the blood supply of the brain, as affected by food and drink, by drugs and vitamins, by the functioning of the glands of internal secretion. All of these items of knowledge lend a cumulative force to the supposition that, when the brain ceases to function, that particular stream of consciousness ceases to exist.

It is just this conclusion, however, which requires a careful examination.

All the facts we have mentioned may be summed up as facts of covariation: change the brain-action and you change the mind; change the mind and you change the brain-action. This fact of covariation, or of the perfect fitting of two sets of changes, implies, of course, that we have two distinguishable sets of changes to deal with. It is the distinguishability which now becomes important.

In order to show what is at stake here, let us take another case of covariation equally exact. A set for a motion picture is being photographed; every slight action, every shadow, every play of expression, is precisely caught by the film. This film could not possibly be the record of any other actors or of any other act than this one. Aristotle's exact correspondence is literally preserved. Yet, if we should argue that there could be no other film record of that set, we should be obviously wrong. Two cameras, at different points, would get numerically different records. Both records would be perfect correspondents to the action, in such wise that they could fit no other set in the universe. But no two corresponding pictures in the two films would be identical. The given mind, to draw our inference, can logically have two different bodies; and if two then more than two, so far as the mere fact of perfect covariation is concerned. It is logically just as possible that the soul should have a plurality of bodies, each of which uniquely fits it, as, that a body should have a plurality of shadows, each of which uniquely fits it, each of them unmistakably the shadow of that person and of no other in the universe.

Aristotle's argument, a good argument against the idea of a soul moving into the body of another person, or into any kind of a misfit body, thus proves to be no argument at all against the idea of a soul having another body or series of bodies, each of which fulfills the requirement of being a precise representation in space of that soul. And all the subsequent arguments which make the picture of fitness more precise are equally incapable of excluding the possibility of a plurality of embodiments of a given mind.

Indeed, I think we may say that we have experiences which,

without amounting to anything like a proof that it is so, vividly indicate to us how this might be.

Persons who dream do not always dream of having a body. That is, they do not always, in their dreams, give attention to the fact that they have bodies. But they frequently dream of moving and acting in situations that imply a body; if one dreams of trying to escape from a pursuer, he may be desperately annoyed by sluggish and disobedient limbs; but his efforts imply that there are limbs and that they are his. And they are certainly not identical with the limbs which are quiescent in the bed. The dream body is in effect another body; yet it is uniquely the body of the dreaming person.

I conclude that this particular scientific objection to the notion of another life vanishes upon careful logical analysis.

The Philosophical Objection

The scientific conviction runs deeper than this formal consideration of fitness. It would be comparatively easy for a scientist to agree that we could imagine the soul to have many bodies, just as we can imagine a given snake to have a series of skins, each of which is peculiar to that individual snake. But to believe in that possibility requires something more than to imagine it. In the case of the snake, the animal produces the skin, not the skin the animal. However, the analogy seems to fail, for in the case of the human being the scientist feels that the body produces the soul, not the soul the body. If the body produces the soul, it is impossible that a given soul could have any other body than the one that produces it. Only if the body is a product of the soul could there be another body for the same soul, in another sphere of existence.

The problem here is one for philosophy, and not for science. The question is: Which is first in being, the body or the soul? (I am here using " soul " and " mind " as equivalent expressions, for the sake of simplicity.)

All the appearances, or most of them, favor the idea that the body is first in existence, and the mind a later development. The process of human reproduction is biological: one would say that what is continuous from parent to child is not the mental life but rather the germ plasm. It is a generally accepted view that the embryo must have a certain degree of development before consciousness arrives — though the moment of that arrival is not one science is prepared to fix, since the fact of consciousness is wholly inaccessible to observation. But the signs of mind, in groping and experimental behavior, appear only as the child approaches the stage of independent bodily existence; they seem to follow from the appropriate development of the nervous system; and they seem to come when they do because the body can then make use of an organ of guidance for its own behavior. All of this, as well as the facts we have already mentioned showing that the condition and vigor of the mind depend on its nutrition and the quality of its blood supply, seems to certify that the mind is present for the sake of the body, as one of its means of survival and guidance, and not the body for the sake of the mind. And, if this is the case, when the body has run its course its particular mind has no more to do; and, as dependent on the body, it can no longer exist.

This, I believe, is the persuasive argument against the continued life of the personal consciousness. It is so obvious, and so in accord with common sense as well as with science, that in its presence the notion of immortality takes on the guise of a pleasant fancy which sober judgment, based on the patent facts, tends to dismiss.

We remember that in the Platonic dialogue *Phaedo*, when Socrates in the prison observes two of his young friends consulting one another during a pause in the discussion, he surmises that they feel his plea for survival to be defective, and are hesitating to press their objections lest, in this, his last day of life, they should be depriving him of at least a comforting hope. It is he, then, who takes the initiative to drive into the open the lurking doubt. Least of all does he, in that hour, wish to go forward under any illusion. In the unique moment of death, which each must face alone, the only firm companion is the truth.

Socrates had suggested that the body was like a musical instrument, the soul like the music; so that the body was for the sake of the soul, not the soul for the sake of the body. But then comes the damaging reflection that, if the instrument is broken, the music also must cease. It is at this point also that our present and modern argument seems to stand, with all the fortification of the scientific demonstrations of dependence. And it is not at once clear that we can derive any light from the consideration by which Socrates revived the argument with his friends. He reminded them that there was one important difference between the instrument-music relationship and the body-soul relationship. The instrument needed some outer person to play it; the soul seemed to initiate its own music — it played itself. That is true; but does not this simply mean, in modern terms, that the body-mind combination is able to initiate its own motions, without external help? It does not imply what we need, namely, that the mind is able to call the body into being, as in a sense the music calls the musical instrument into being.

And if the mind were able to call the body into being, would we not know it? whereas, is it not the reverse that we are aware of in our inner consciousness — that our minds are frail things, flickering with every wind of health and illness, vigor or fatigue, and, when the physical basis is too disturbed, flickering out?

This, I think, is the crucial point in the philosophical inquiry into immortality. Is it true that the mind depends upon the body, and not the body on the mind? If so, immortality is excluded.

But a closer look seems to show that both things are true. Of course, we must take our food in order to keep on thinking;

but also we must think in order to take our food. Of course, we may speed up our thinking if we so desire by a cup of coffee; but the body does not take the cup of coffee without the prior decision of the mind. To say in such cases that the state of the mind depends on the body is to say only half the truth; the whole truth is that the state of mind at the present moment depends on what the mind in a previous moment decided to do to itself by way of the body. The body was a necessary means for working out the mind's own wishes for its future condition. The initiative lay wholly with the mind.

And in the course of years of this submission to the mind's dictation, the body is modified, or even made over: it becomes more completely the mind's instrument. It has been said that at fifteen a woman begins to show the beauty that nature gives her; at fifty she shows the beauty that she gives herself. There is much truth in this, for at fifty the constant working of the character into the attitudes and expressions of the body tell an unmistakable story; and, if this simple truth were better known by the women of America, their artificial methods of achieving beauty might give way to something far more substantial and — may one say — far more effective.

If I were to correct that statement it would only be by way of questioning what it says about the beauty of youth and childhood: that this is what nature gives, and not the self. I would rather say that the early beauty of the human body is what the mind accepts, the later beauty is what it fashions. As I look more closely at the relation between mind and body in childhood, I would not say that the mind at that time is more at the mercy of the body. I would say that the earlier period is one of *docility*, the later period one of *command*. The child is at a stage in which nutrition is the dominant impulse and necessity; but the nutrition is both mental and physical. The child is docile toward its entire social surrounding; it is highly content to be itself; it has no quarrel to pick with its ancestry, with its race, color, shape or condition; it desires simply to be more of the same — that is, to grow. It has to find out what this person is it calls itself, and what it is like as compared with others; it is becoming acquainted, through the mirrors of social life, with the self which it knows at first only as an intimate and somewhat formless center of consciousness and action.

At the same time it is becoming acquainted with its visible body. The child does not at first see its body; it only feels it, as a mass of sensation, comfortable or uncomfortable, and with various possibilities of action, bringing about changes in sensation. This is as much as to say that the body, for the child, is at first a part of its conscious mind. To say that it accepts this consciously felt body is simply to say that it accepts itself; and, if that body seems to an outer observer to have beauty, that beauty is not in any exclusive sense the beauty which " Nature " has given — it is also the beauty of that inner self, in its early harmony. There is nothing in this situation that requires us to say the body is first, and the mind a product. Both develop in complete accord. The facts would be quite as well satisfied by a hypothesis which to my mind is far nearer the truth: that the body is simply the visible symbol of the mind. And if the will has an influence over the body in later life, as it certainly has, it is probable that it has at least as much influence over the body in childhood. Only, in childhood, the influence of the will should be more completely subconscious, because, in the period of docility, the child has less capacity to criticize the sort of being it is, and has therefore less conscious motive to make itself over.

I reach therefore this general result, that throughout life the body depends on the mind, even while the mind is dependent in other respects upon the body.

With this result we are, so to speak, halfway emancipated from the notion that the mind is so far a slave of the body that if the body dies the mind must die also. We reach the point of seeing the mind as at least an equal partner in the destiny of the person. But it is only a halfway emancipation. What we have is a familiar sort of interdependence; A depends on B and B depends on A. In this sort of mutuality, there is no assurance that if one of the members drops away the other can continue to exist.

It would be possible to point out that with the growth to maturity the period of command replaces the period of docility and the body becomes increasingly subject to the will of its owner. It becomes increasingly natural for the soul to refer to " my body " and increasingly unnatural for the body to refer to " my mind "! But then it has also to be admitted that with advancing age the mind seems to lose its ascendency, and the infirmities of the body begin to impede its own self-command.

We should do better to inquire in what respect we have to say that the mind is dependent on the body, and in what respect it is not dependent.

It is customary to think of the dependence of the mind on the body in three main ways. First, it is said we require the body to keep us informed of the outer world through sensation, especially through sight and hearing. Second, it is said we require the body to give us an active effect on the outer world through the motor nerves and the muscles: without this we would be helpless spectators of events, able to think but not to will. Third, it is said we require the energy of the brain to supply the energy of thought.

I am not sure that any of these statements is exact.

Ordinarily we seem to see by way of our eyes; but then our eyes are one of the things we see. And if we only know of our eyes by way of our eyes, there is a chance we may be mistaken about that necessity. We dream fairly well when our eyes are shut. And Beethoven set music before his mind long after his ears were soundless. It is not absolutely certain that we require eyes and ears for seeing and hearing — though we do require them for keeping in touch with certain sources of light and sound we call external. As for the energy of thought, it does not seem to be in any clear relation to the physical energy of the brain: the best intelligence is not the intelligence that has to strain hardest to get an idea, but the intelligence that grasps the idea without effort. Farsightedness seems to be a function of mental balance rather than of mental strain. There is no known way of stoking the mental engines so that a slow wit will become even moderately bright; and no dosing with iodine or any other known drug will turn a moderate ability into a genius, though there are drugs that may produce the sad illusion of genius.

But, allowing the body in all these matters the benefit of such doubt as there is, we may say that the body appears to be the agency of connection between one person and the " outside world " which consists primarily of another group of persons. The connective tissue between members of a community is what we call the physical world of " Nature." Nature is common property for all of us; we have the same space and time, the same earth and stars, the same geological history. We do not see one another's minds; but we see bodies which we learn to identify with the minds of others. The body is first of all the means of identification that other people use for any given person; the body symbolizes the person. Then, as that body seems to use its eyes and ears, we assume that the person symbolized by it is conscious of the same world with us, and may be apprehending the signals we issue. As the body acts, we assume that the person is using volition to effect changes in his own position, or changes in the world outside him. All this sums up in the proposition that the body is a means of communication between one person and other persons by way of a common physical world.

It is also, of course, a means of receiving communications and effects. You arrest a person by arresting his body; you fight him by fighting his body; if you injure his body you injure him; if he demands a court hearing you grant him the use of his body, " habeas corpus."

But in all of this one thing has not been said. It has not been said that we require the body in order to exist. Until someone comes forward with an explanation of how it would be possible for a body to produce a mind, the assertion that the body develops or evolves the mind connected with it remains both unfounded and unintelligible. With all the ingenuity of scientific hypothesis, it has to be said that no advance whatever has been made since Aristotle or before in answering the question how, from a mindless universe, or a mindless organism, a mind could emerge. (I use the word " emerge " intentionally, because I wish to include " emergent evolution " explicitly among the hypotheses which are intended to relieve the mystery, and which completely fail to do so.)

But for the opposite question — " How can the body depend on the mind for its existence? " — there is at least one definite item of evidence. That is found in the everyday experience of decision. In the act of deciding a course of action between several alternatives, it is necessary that each alternative shall be imagined as a future possibility. We can choose between going into dairy farming or into woodcutting only if both of these occupations are available to us; and only one of them can happen. Our minds are busy with prophetic pictures; we see ourselves surrounded by our future herd, or by the grimmer scenes of the winter forest; we see the paths leading to each of these scenes. All the past momenta of Nature lead up to the moment in which I now stand facing these alternatives; but they do not carry me through that moment. I halt the impetuosity of Nature until I am ready to decide. Then I insert into the causal runways of Nature the special actions that will carry me along one path or the other, to the dairy farm or to the winter forest. And when the chosen picture arrives it will be I, and not Nature, that made it real; and yet — and here is the point — it has become a part of Nature. And without me, and my imagination, it could never have come to pass. It is my mind, in what we call a free choice, upon which that particular bit of the physical world depends, and, within it, the activity of my body which belongs with it. Here the very existence of that phase of the bodily life depends on the prior mental act of choice.

The implications of this fact, partial as it may seem, are momentous: If the human mind or soul is capable of what we call a free choice, it is, in that small chink of the universe, standing for a moment outside the stream of cause and effect and determining what Nature shall contain. In principle, the body is there dependent on the mind, not the mind on the body.

And if this is the case in that small chink of the universe, we have there an insight into the way things are put together. We can see that in its own character the physical world, which destroys the body, cannot destroy what is free from the body.

The death of the body, if we are right, would be the cessation (or the symbol of the cessation) of a set of connections with a particular community of other persons. There would remain the possibility that the inner energy of the self, if it had attained to the self-command which would give its continuance a meaning, would enable it to make connections with other such communities. And in so doing it would find itself with another body, exactly fitting its own individual character, identifying it in its relations with that new environment.

So far, we find that the philosophical objection to the idea of immortality does not hold good. Like the scientific objection, it leaves the field free for any ground of a more positive nature that we may have to justify a belief in that further dimension of the universe.

The Ground for Belief

No one, I think, is likely to come to a belief in immortality through argument. It is the work of argument to remove obstacles, not to bring positive conviction. The argument is necessary because no one living in a scientific age can fairly remain indifferent to the view of man that science suggests; he must listen to it and settle his accounts with it. But he must not expect it to provide the answer.

The answer must come directly from personal experience.

But how can there be a personal experience of immortality — that is, of something that relates to a future time, and to a time beyond the limits of human life?

This question which seems quite natural to the American mind would appear unnecessarily stupid to a Hindu or a Buddhist. The object of the Hindu's meditation is to achieve what he calls a " realization " of truth, and of one truth in particular, the truth that in his deepest self he is identical with the source of all being, Brahma or God. To realize this is to know that the accidents of earthly existence — even the deepest of accidents, which is death — cannot destroy the self, any more than night — which is the accident of a shadow — can destroy the sun.

Any personal experience that can show us clearly how things are put together in this universe — what is superior and what is inferior, what the soul is and how it is related to its body, what death is, what it can do and what it cannot do — any experience, I say, that lights up in a flash the articulation of this living world may give us even now an outlook on the future.

C. F. Andrews, friend of Gandhi and of many others, has written of experiences of his own — in connection with the approach to death of two of his nearest friends — that led him to the conviction of immortality. " Truth," he wrote, " is never wholly gained until it becomes individual and personal. An inner conviction has now come to me. There is now a certainty within me that our Spirit is independent and survives all change."

He had in mind one of Gandhi's fasts in which Gandhi came very near to death:

His suffering had become almost unbearable. . . . His mind also seemed under a cloud and he spoke with great difficulty. . . . I questioned him whether he was conscious inwardly of the joy in the spiritual life about which he had spoken before. His face lighted up again immediately, and his answer in the affirmative was emphatic. . . . It came to me with a new power of understanding that the spirit of man is in some way independent of the mind, and in a real sense immortal. . . . It appears to be distinct from the mental process, which is more closely connected with the body.

At the end of his story Andrews quotes from another remarkable Indian, Sadhu Sundar Singh, who had found during a fast of his own that " as his body became weaker his spiritual faculties became more active and alert " and had drawn the inference

that the spirit was something altogether apart from the brain. " The brain," he said, " is like an organ and the spirit like the organist that plays on it. Two or three notes may go wrong and produce no music. That does not however imply the absence of the organist." [3]

(Here, Andrews is using the word " spirit " for what we have called the deeper self.)

Such experiences are not uncommon. They come to us in different ways. They are likely to be such individual perceptions that they mean everything to the one who has them and little to anyone else. Some people I have known have become persuaded of immortality through the very thing which would seem likely to rob them of that belief — the death of a wife or husband. I had a letter some time ago from an old friend, a skeptical and hard-headed naturalist, who had lost his wife. He said:

I have never taken any stock in the notion of any one living after death. It is too contrary to everything that we biologists seem to see with our eyes. But when X died, I suddenly realized that as biologists we *see nothing that touches the question at all.* We see the body die; and we think of life as a property of the body. But consciousness and personality we do not see; they are not the same as organic life. I have a feeling deeper than any argument, not affected by argument, that X cannot have vanished from the universe.

[3] C. F. Andrews, "The Organ and the Organist," *The Christian Century,* LI (1934), 1094. Reprinted by permission.

Such a statement can hardly be persuasive to anyone who has not gone through a similar experience, and yet it is probable that a similar revulsion against the claim of death to have conquered life explains the widespread belief in survival among all races of mankind.

More common is the experience or illusion of partial detachment from the body, in which the body appears as something semi-alien to oneself, an experience that occurs sometimes in deep revery, and sometimes in illness or convalescence. The experience is variously reported as that of being free from one's body, or of observing it as from outside. The significance of such experiences lies not in the question whether they are illusory as particular events, but in the incidental discovery that the self need not be identified with this particular body in order to be itself. In its most general meaning, it is a discovery which anyone can make at any time — that of the inner plurality of the self. For, when one thinks of oneself, or observes or judges oneself, there is immediately a distinction between the self that observes and the self that is observed. Suppose someone has done something of which he is afterward ashamed, and suppose him busied with the remembrance of that deed and his regret at having done it. The *judged* self is condemned and repudiated by the *judging* self, though the weakness that led to that act is still present. The self that is caught in the meshes of habit, heredity, passion, is haled before the court of a self that knows what ought to be and holds that standard free from the deflections of time and circumstance. One might say perhaps that the eternal self is judging the temporal and experimental self. Both selves are required to make up the complete and humanly living self, but the self which (as Plato would put it) participates in the true standards of judgment can be seen to have a deeper lodgment in the nature of things than the self of these experimental excursions. It is more " real."

And it is interesting to observe that when the human being thinks about his own death, and of the time after his death when he will no longer be present among men — an act of reflection which men often perform, and which in all probability animals never perform — he has to imagine this reflective self as continuing to live; otherwise it could not observe the absence of the visible self from among the living. The thought of annihilation can never be completely executed, because self-consciousness must remain in order to attempt to execute it.

From such experiences and reflections, many have come to the clear personal perception that — as they would put it — the true self cannot be destroyed by the crisis of death, for its position is such that it rides above that crisis.

This conviction gives them a further answer to the question that we earlier raised, about the possibility of the free sacrifice of life for a cause, which we find so common today in the armies of materialistic societies. Indeed that willingness to die is present wherever we have human nature at its best, as in the pursuit of new paths in medicine and in other phases of science and its applications. There never have been wanting men who were ready to die for the sake of man. For, as we now see, in freely rejecting life, there is a self that is rejected and a self that rejects. In rejecting life for the sake of a higher good, the self that rejects unconsciously lays hold on what is more valuable, and more durable, than the life itself that is rejected.

But there is a third type of experience more common, I believe, than either of these. It is the realization that there must be purpose in the universe as a whole; and that the annihilation of the spirit of man in death would, by canceling the meaning of things, amount to the denial of purpose. For somehow the aspiring and questioning human soul, weak as it is, embodies all that we can see of the significance of creation. The world is vast and man is puny; but unless the vast world knows itself and its meaning, it is less real than petty man, who *does* know himself and his unending craving for finding the meaning of his life in space and time.

That living spark, just because it is inquiring and seeking, just because it raises the question of futility which a dead universe cannot raise, just because it is capable of suffering at the spectacle of an infinite waste of insensate matter, is more *real* than any such waste could be. And, seeing this, one apprehends at once as by a swift flash of light that — since the more real cannot be obliterated by the less real — the soul that aspires cannot be obliterated by death.

7

"TO WHOM WILL YE LIKEN GOD?"

Charles E. Park

CHARLES E. PARK recently retired from the position he had held for forty years as minister of the First Church in Boston (Unitarian). A fellow of the American Academy of Arts and Sciences, Dr. Park also serves as secretary of the Franklin Foundation of Boston. His most recent book is *Christianity: How It Came to Us; What It Is; What It Might Be.*

7 *Charles E. Park*

"TO WHOM WILL YE LIKEN GOD?"[1]

O
UR IDEA OF God is determined by two
considerations: what we are, and what we need. The Creator
reveals himself in his creation. Self-knowledge gives us the
only clue we have to the nature and qualities of our Creator.
Of recent centuries we have come to know an increasing
amount about the planet on which we live, about other forms
of life that share this planet with us, about the solar system of
which our planet is a member and about the eight or nine other
planets, big and little, who are our fellow members in this particular solar system. This knowledge is constantly growing.
It is now a respectable mass of evidence from which to derive
at least the beginnings of our idea of God. On the principle
that the thing created cannot be greater than the power that
created it, we must derive from this mass of evidence an idea
of God that shall think of him as the original cause of all we
know we are, and all we know our fellow creatures and our
world and our universe are.

This is not all, though: there is also the knowledge of what
we want to be, and hope to be. To separate man from his aspirations is to leave a mere fragment of the man. One of the qualities that mark man from other forms of life is his ability to
extend the context of his self-consciousness into past and
future; to find his satisfaction never wholly in the present, but

[1] Delivered at Lancaster, Pennsylvania, as the Garvin Lecture for 1946, under
the title, "The Idea of God as Affected by Modern Knowledge."

partly in memory and partly in hope. What he has been and
what he plans to be are just as important to the man as what he
is. Our idea of God, therefore, must be fashioned to explain
not only what man has been and is, but what he may be in days
to come. God must be the thought in which we find adequate
explanation for the facts of our existence as they are realized
at this present, and as they may be realized in the future.

When we consider how stupendous those facts are, we get
a rather impressive idea of the conceptual task we are under-
taking. An old minister had the habit of once a year preaching
a sermon in which he summarized the advances in astronomy
of that year. He did this, he said, " because it greatly enlarges
my idea of God." That is precisely the effect it has on our
minds to glance over the tremendous field of human living as
it lies in man's knowledge. The thing created is seen to be so
enormous that it necessitates a greatly enlarged idea of its
Creator. As we consider the further adjustments in our idea
of the Creator that a still increasing creation promises to require
at our hands, we ask ourselves if it is ever going to be possible
for our human minds to formulate anything like an adequate
idea of such a Creator. We may as well reconcile ourselves to
failure. Sometimes it seems as if the more our knowledge of
his created world and of his creature man increases, the further
he himself recedes from the grasp of our understanding.

Thus we are in a position to make the first general statement
upon the question of how the idea of God is affected by modern
knowledge. Modern knowledge has tremendously enlarged
our idea of God. As modern knowledge increases it bids fair
to render an adequate idea of God even less possible than it has
been in the past. This, however, does not excuse us from the
task of formulating such an idea. Furthermore, modern knowledge has gone far enough to warn us of its own limitations.
That is to say, we know enough about ourselves to realize that
our idea of God must aim to satisfy more than just the knowing
part of us. It must aim to satisfy the whole creature, Man — his

feelings, his volition, his intuition, his aspirations, his purposefulness, his spiritual cravings and hopes, his rationality as a balanced and integrated whole of manhood, as well as that strictly knowing part of him we call his mind. Modern knowledge, therefore, comes to us with a tacit and rather generous recommendation: Remember that I, Knowledge, am but one way of approach to the thought of God. There are other ways to employ in formulating your idea of God which have just as good a claim to your respect as I have, and which can take you farther and help you more than I can. Do not confine yourself to me. Use your intuition, your imagination, your speculative ability, your spiritual hunger and thirst. Remember that God is the great quest not only for Christians, but for all men of every class and sect and religious affiliation. Therefore, in forming your idea of God, step outside your traditional Christian experience and avail yourself of all human experience, Jewish, Greek, Hindu, Chinese and Egyptian. Remember again that the search for God is not recent; it is as old as mankind. Do not hesitate to use the thought-habits of former ages as well as those of this current age.

This is a very timely and valuable recommendation, and thoroughly in keeping with the character and spirit of modern knowledge. We speak rather glibly of " modern knowledge," but just what do we mean by it? For one thing, of course, we mean recent knowledge; knowledge brought down to date by the addition of the latest discoveries, the latest observations of phenomena, and the latest adjustments of theory and hypothesis as rendered necessary by those latest discoveries and observations. But modern knowledge must be something more than recent knowledge. The psychologist Dr. Carl Gustav Jung, in his book, *Modern Man in Search of a Soul,* says that the modern man is the conscious man. He lives in the present, but he is consciously aware of all the forces, discoveries, failures, achievements and experiences that have made this present what it is. The modern man is a great deal more than the contemporaneous man; he is the man who harbors a consciousness of the whole history of human trial and error in the past, as well as a consciousness of the merely contemporaneous fads and fashions that strive to determine his life in this present.

We can say the same about modern knowledge. The knowledge that holds within its conscious attention the entire surviving body of all past knowledge in addition to the body of contemporaneous knowledge is modern knowledge. Hence the concept of God as affected by modern knowledge is the concept of God as affected by the sum total of valid human knowledge whether acquired in past ages or in recent months. It is very important to guard ourselves from serious injustice to the past, because the achievements of past ages are worthy of the profoundest respect we can show. This hateful habit of sneering at any item of man's knowledge that is more than fifty years old can lead us into error. We do well to remember that human minds three thousand years ago were not only just as competent as human minds today but, for theological purposes, better qualified and more competent than our minds today. They had far more of the philosophical habit and far less of the scientific habit of thinking than we.

When you bought your ticket on the steamer that used to run between Boston and Bangor, you were asked if you would have an outside or an inside stateroom; in making your choice you betrayed certain interesting facts about yourself — whether yours was the broadly speculative or the closely analytical type of mind. Here was the steamer, a fairly well differentiated, self-sufficient microcosm in itself. If you found it more interesting to follow the fortunes of the steamer as a whole in her relation to other objects and natural features around her, you would choose an outside stateroom. Then you could sit at your open window and trace the course of the steamer as she felt her way to her destination. On the other hand, if you were willing to leave the steamer and its proper navigation to the captain in the pilot house, and felt that your real interest was in the life that goes on within a steamer, you would choose an inside stateroom. Then you could sit at your open window and look in upon the activities of the huge saloon. The outside stateroom symbolizes your taste for speculation. The inside stateroom symbolizes your taste for analysis.

Substituting the true terms in this allegory, we think of this planet, Earth, with its two billion human passengers making its voyage through the dark oceans of eternity, and discover the same two points of view represented by the outside and the inside staterooms. When man first began to think, he was probably far more of a speculative than an analytic thinker. He had to be alert to his surroundings if he wanted to keep alive. All his dangers came upon him from the outside — winds, rain, cold, blizzards, wild beasts of the forest and hostile marauders from the next valley. These dangers had to have his attention, for his survival depended on his alertness to the perils around him, and on his ability to speculate what they were going to do before they did it. So man developed as a speculative thinker. His steamboat of human life had only one kind of stateroom, the outside stateroom.

We are not surprised then, as the generations rolled along, and as the mind of man reached its full competence, to see the great age of metaphysical speculation upon the nature of God and the human soul. We cannot say when or where that age began. All we know is that at about the same time, from five hundred to a thousand years before Christ, in China, India, Persia, Palestine, Greece and Egypt, men began to dream the mightiest dreams and see the brightest visions that have ever dawned upon human consciousness. Their efforts to put these visions of God into words still leave us baffled and mystified. The Chinese tried to conceive of God as the Way, the Persians as the Light, the Hindus as the Eternal Tranquillity, the Greeks as Pure Thought, the Hebrews as Holy Purpose. All used the most splendid words their language afforded, only to find that the splendor of their thought could not be crowded into words. When we read what they have written the clearest and strongest impression we get is that they are trying to tell us something that reaches beyond the utmost range of human language. They are trying to tell us that there is a Wonderful Something back of our life, too vast to be understood, too elusive to be captured, too holy to be described. We despair of gaining any clear concept; we can only look in the direction they indicate.

This age of speculation reached its height centuries before Christ. It is a height that human thought has never surpassed, and finds it difficult even now to scale. How long the age lasted we cannot say, perhaps a thousand, perhaps fifteen hundred years. Gradually there came a change in man's habit of thought. The fear of Christ's second coming to inaugurate a final judgment day little by little wore off. This earth continued to exist in spite of all forebodings, and even gave promise of lasting indefinitely. Therefore it was worthy of a better acquaintance and a closer analysis. What kind of a place was this world? What were its laws, qualities, dangers and opportunities? And what kind of a creature was this being called Man who lived on this earth? What were his powers and weaknesses, his aversions and ambitions? How could this man get the most out of his life on this earth? Such questions invited an introspective, self-analyzing habit of mind. So human life was put on a more solid earthly basis. Cathedrals took the place of early churches. Monasteries dedicated to prayer and intercession developed into universities and became centers of learning. The revival of learning followed with its first groping steps into the field of science, and its first timid experiments in chemistry, physics and biology. Great discoveries were made that increased man's health and length of days, and gave him the beginnings of his growing mastery over the forces of nature. Before he knew it, man had shifted his point of attention from the world around him to the world within him. He had exchanged his outside stateroom for an inside stateroom.

This hasty glance backward over the history of human thought reveals a significant fact. We can see that for the early part of the last three thousand years human minds were chiefly interested in speculating on the nature and disposition of the outside world, the forces surrounding man. We have seen that these speculations constitute a permanent and a priceless achievement commanding the highest respect of all later generations. We can also see that, during the latter part of this three-thousand-year period, man's habit of thought has changed from being chiefly speculative to being chiefly analytical, as his attention has been shifted from the forces of life around him to the forces of life within him. This means only that the nature of his thinking has been changed from the philosophical to the scientific. And it is only fair to say that his more recent achievements in the fields of science are just as remarkable in their way as the achievements of the ancient speculators. If we must feel the profoundest respect for what they did, they must feel just as profound a respect for what we have done and are still doing. The thing to remember is that neither achievement has any right to overshadow the other, or to claim a greater importance than the other. In the composition of modern knowledge the speculative range of the ancients must be given just as important a place in consciousness as the analytical precision of the present day, and any idea of God that refuses to acknowledge the influence of that speculative range of former times is no more modern than it would be if it refused to feel the influence of the analytical precision of these recent times.

The whole secret of modern knowledge is the ability to gather up into conscious attention the entire period of man's mental discipline, and then glean from this wide and varied field its harvest of achievement. That harvest must constitute the *continuum* we call modern knowledge. There will be items that, we say, we must discard because they have been fundamentally discredited by subsequent discoveries. Yet even the discards would better be made humbly and hypothetically; for, to tell the truth, we do not yet know just what to discard. We cannot yet be sure but what some new discovery or observation will suddenly bring into sharp focus and invest with vital significance some fantastic belief, like the transmutation of metals, which has long been ridiculed as a grotesque fallacy. Our only safeguard is a great humility.

In precisely this direction modern knowledge has of recent years been influencing our idea of God: that is, recapturing and revitalizing certain concepts that we had too hastily discarded. Suppose we glance at a few of these rehabilitated concepts.

Reading the Old Testament we are left in no doubt as to who is the real hero of the story: God himself, Jehovah, Lord God of Sabaoth, who strides through every page and dominates every situation, whose praise or blame is of the first consequence to mortal man. In his majestic anthropomorphisms we trace the lineaments of a being who is enough like man to justify the assertion that man is created in his image and after his likeness. Yet, the strongest impression we get is the impression of his Otherness. He is the Great Not-man, the Other than man, separated from man by degrees of superiority that constitute an impassable chasm. There is no ontological or metaphysical identity between this God and the lesser forms of life. To be sure, he created the world and living creatures including man, but he still remains distinct from his creation, a wholly separate Being, of greater power, larger heart, abler mind and loftier point of view. Human history is the record of man's traffic with this rather terrible being. In that traffic God shows himself always the imperious and exacting sovereign, the watchful and censorious judge, a terror to evildoers, a blessing to the righteous, sometimes a defense and a champion who rewards his faithful with a word of approval, sometimes a hindrance and a nuisance who interrupts human designs with his arbitrary objections and upsets the best-laid plans with his angry disapproval. But he is always distinct from man, another being, who must be taken into account first, the first to be obeyed, or placated, or deceived, or evaded, or somehow circumvented, depending on the timidity or the recklessness of the man himself. This God was not only the greatest of all gods, he was the only God. The Old Testament rises to a triumphant monotheism, but this monotheism is not to be confused with the monism of the Hindus. The one and only God of the Jews is still distinct from his creation. He is one member in a dualism, the other member of which is mankind.

This trick of dualistic thinking is deeply rooted in our Christian minds. It is our inheritance from the Old Testament, and has become instinctive. We think of God, heaven, eternity and holiness as concepts forming a class by themselves. We set them in clear-cut contradistinction to man, earth, time and secularity, which form an entirely separate class of concepts. The result of this trick of thought is obvious. As we pry into the secrets of nature, try to understand the composition of the world, the structure and method of human life and behavior, we discover that everything that takes place, every change and reaction, can be traced to the operation of certain great quiet inexorable laws, the laws of compensation, gravity, centrifugal force, atomic affinity, conservation of energy and the like. Apparently, when God created our solar system he also created a code of laws to control its behavior. When he created life on one of these planets, he created a code of laws to control this mystery called life in all its combinations, developments and evolutions. Under the operation of these laws the germ of life has sought ever larger and more differentiated forms, and has gradually taken on the form of human beings and human societies. In all this process of evolution we can detect no spot at which God has interfered to halt or to deflect the operation of these laws. Having once created the world and set it going under the management of these laws, what is there left for God to do? What necessary place does he hold, or what essential function does he perform in a world that is steadily slipping along in the ways dictated to it by the unbreakable laws of its creation and subsequent behavior? Would it not be more to the point to worship those laws, for are they not the power that controls our fortunes? God has nothing to do with our fate now. Every item of that fate is determined by law. Where does God fit into a world, once it is created and set going? How are we to think of him? How can we say that he answers to any need of ours?

Ever since Descartes first asked that question three hundred years ago, men have engaged in a frantic search for some way to fit God into his creation, some necessary place for him to occupy in the system of life he once upon a time created. Some of the answers proposed are downright comical, they are so naïve. One favorite answer is to equate God with that which we do not yet understand. God is the algebraic x, the Unknown Property. The physicist says, " There must be a form of matter even more simple and elementary than the electron. We don't know what it is; we will call it God." The astronomer says, " There must be a combination of life-forms even more majestic than the supergalaxy. We don't know what it is; suppose we call it God." The biologist says, " There must be some answer to this quantum theory, some arbitrary power to tell these molecules to combine in one cell on a basis of mutual helpfulness, for that is the only kind of cell that can survive. Happy thought: there is something for God to do." The historian says, " There must have been some supervising genius to keep Napoleon in complete ignorance of the sunken road at Waterloo. Who can doubt it was the work of God?"

What a convenience that concept of God has been — still is, in fact — to thousands of pseudo scientists and thousands of mechanistic thinkers! Just as handy as a pocket in a shirt. They construct their little cosmic system. It is so harmonious and so self-sufficient in its interrelationships of cause and effect that it really has no place for God. But as it happens the system is not yet perfect; there is a gap in it. Never mind. They can fill up the gap with God, just as you would stuff up the holes in a barrel full of crockery with a wad of excelsior, until you can find something better to put in that hole, some little mechanistic reason or relationship that really belongs there, and that you had overlooked. Then with a whoop of delight, out comes God and in goes the missing part. Finally the system is perfected. The last element is found. The last link in the chain of causation is discovered. There is no more need for the excelsior to take up the loose play and stop the rattle. The whole system is tight as a drum, and God is out of a job!

This concept of God as a substitute for the unknown quantity, a temporary makeshift to take up the slack until the missing part can be found, has a surprising currency among thousands of superficial scientists who do not know what speculative thinking is, and who have been misled by the slant of thought inherited from the Old Testament: that God is a being separate from his creation. It is at this point that modern knowledge makes its first and perhaps its greatest correction. Look beyond your recent times, says modern knowledge, look beyond your strictly Christian traditions of thought and concept. Men were doing some magnificent thinking even before Christ. The writers of the Old Testament were not the only metaphysicians. Take your stand upon the summit of all human achievement. Then see for yourself that you cannot put the cart before the horse. You cannot fit God as a distinct factor into a pre-existent creation. God comes first. If there is a creation, God must be thought of as the Creator. If you discover a self-justifying system of cause and effect, God is the Maker. If you can recognize a self-maintaining equilibrium of forces, God is the builder. Everything that is must have a cause. God is the primal cause, himself uncaused. Your task is not to fit God into his own creation, but to fit creation into God's thought and plan; not to separate God from the world and mankind, but to find the world and mankind in God, impregnated with his creative will, sustained from moment to moment by his power, regulated at every point by his law, and justified by his purpose.

Our concept of God as influenced by modern knowledge is thus losing none of its monotheistic quality, but is taking on more and more of the quality of monism. Modern knowledge, especially of recent years, is becoming more and more of a world-wide freemasonry, both in its geographic and in its chronological dimension. It is striving more and more to include within its treasure chamber the worthy and valid things that have been done not only in all countries but in all ages. If it is true, as Whittier says, that

> In all lands beneath the sun
> The heart affirmeth Love is one,

it is equally true that in all lands beneath the sun the mind affirmeth Truth is one. We must admit the greatest hazard modern knowledge has had to overcome has been a sort of intellectual nationalism or even parochialism, which tempts people to flatter themselves that the only learning worth having is their own, that they are the world's most intellectual, most enlightened people, that all others are inferior. The best thing modern knowledge has done is to break down this barrier of self-complacency and insist that the experience and observation of other peoples, ancient as well as contemporary, may be considered just as valid as our own, and may be held in equal respect and included as a valuable item in the august body of knowledge that is available to the world of this day. This tendency toward intellectual broadmindedness has a special significance for our present interest. A study of comparative religion is of the highest value to us in formulating our concept of God; for if our world is ever to be drawn together into what the late Wendell Willkie called " One World," then the first point of attention is the world's religion. We can hardly hope as yet to see the world adopting one religion, but we can hope to form a concept of God that shall be a sort of greatest common factor in all religions, and shall have world-wide acceptability. Modern knowledge helps us to form such a concept just because modern knowledge is beginning to show a willingness to include within itself the best experience and reflection of all races and ages. If we can conceive of God in ways that shall command the respect of Asiatics, Hindus, Russians, Jews, Arabs and Europeans, as well as ourselves, we shall take a long step toward the attainment of lasting peace. Fortunately all the influence of modern knowledge is in that direction. God, the monistic Principle of life, the Primal Being, the Uncaused Cause of all that is, the Great River of conscious existence of whose body and spirit all our known creation is a part, fashioned by him, sustained by him, governed by his laws, instruments of his purpose — such a concept can be labeled Chinese, Brahmin, Zoroastrian, Greek, Mohammedan, Jewish or Christian. There is nothing in that concept to offend the real scientist, and there is nothing to disappoint the metaphysician.

Such a concept of God is precisely the concept to which modern knowledge offers the least objection; or, to put it in a better way, it is the concept to which modern knowledge holds out the greatest hospitality and encouragement. This concept not only utilizes our recent scientific interest in spiritual values; it also utilizes the learning of former generations in its speculative range and daring. It not only acknowledges the influence of our strictly Christian experience and tradition, but where that Christian bias is seen to be a narrowing and distorting influence it corrects it by making room for the achievements of the great non-Christian or pre-Christian thinkers. This concept contains the answer to the spiritual needs of the Brahmin and the Buddhist, in whose eyes this earth is nothing but an endless, meaningless, futile wheel of rebirths that gets you nowhere, and whose chief religious aim is to find some way of escape from this ever-revolving wheel of rebirths; it also contains the answer to the healthier and more optimistic craving of the Christian, which is a craving for some justifying objective: in the words of Tennyson, some

> far-off divine event,
> To which the whole creation moves.

To state this concept is no easy task, but some attempt at such a statement must be made.

As we have seen, this concept is not satisfied to think of God as a demiurge, one of several demiurges, who finds creation already in existence, and who must then be fitted into the scheme of things, and given a function worthy of his dignity. God must be conceived as the Creator; he comes before creation, not after; he is the primal cause; there can be no cause antecedent to him. Moreover, this concept is not satisfied with mere monotheism, and not satisfied to think of God as a supernatural being who at a certain point in our stream of time created this world while keeping himself distinct from this world, a being of a different order. That dualism of thought which recognizes two kinds of life, the natural and the supernatural, is not popular with modern knowledge. " Life is life which generates, and many-seeming life is one."

According to our concept, then, God is the monistic Principle of Life, in all its forms and degrees: the ever-active Creativity; the Universal Mind; the ever-flowing river of Being; the eternally purposeful thought-substance in constant search of more adequate self-expression. He created all that is, and includes within his Being all that is. That is to say, he realizes himself in creation, or creation is simply his self-realization. " For in him we live, and move, and have our being," because he lives and moves in us and includes us as part of his being. We say that our world is enveloped by a layer of gases which we call our atmosphere, and which supports life. This atmosphere rests upon us as an invisible pressure of about fifteen pounds to the square inch, both inside and out, and our organs and tissues are so constructed as to require that pressure and to withstand it without conscious effort. The only way to make us conscious of that pressure is to take us out of it — carry us up in an airplane into the stratosphere where we suffer and perish for lack of it. God is a kind of atmosphere within whose pressure we must remain if we want to live. We are so constructed that we are completely unconscious of that life-sustaining pressure until we are taken out of it. Then we suffer and perish. That pressure contains all that we need to live. It made possible our life in the first instance. It supports our life from moment to moment. It is within us as well as without. It is the momentary cause of all we are or have or know. We are held in suspension within that atmosphere, but we do not exhaust it. A fragment of God is allocated in our being, but there is a great deal of God left over when we have absorbed all of the divine vitality we need. The supply is inexhaustible. God lives both within us and round about us, both in others and all about. He is both immanent and transcendent — like an ever-burning fire, always giving off of himself, but never himself diminished.

We have therefore, as the basis of our concept of God, this thought of the monistic Life-principle. To this basic concept we can add other attributes and qualities. On the supposition that the thing created cannot be more than the power that creates it, we can examine our own spiritual powers and find in them indications of the qualities we may postulate of God's nature. We cannot argue away this supposition. To say that the germ of life in the creature can develop into differentiations that are not to be discovered in the Creator is to say that something can come from nothing. To say that all the oak tree lies in the acorn may not be easy. Yet something like that has got to be said. The acorn must contain within itself the biological potentials that ultimately produce the full-grown monarch of the forest. We have to think of God either as eternally perfected Being or as even now Becoming, still in process of perfecting himself in the creation in which he embodies himself. It makes little difference whether we think of him one way or the other, Being or Becoming. In either case, what we are still has its significance and its influence on our concept of him. We cannot put ourselves on a higher plane than God. If, like Emerson, we think

> Of Caesar's hand, and Plato's brain,
> Of Lord Christ's heart, and Shakespeare's strain . . .

as samples of human power and excellence, then, whether God is Being or Becoming, that much at least God is. If we can claim for ourselves the wondrous qualities of intelligence, memory, hope and the like, then, whether as Complete Being who has always possessed them, or as Incomplete Becoming who acquires them through our acquisition, we have got to say these qualities are in God. Our possession of them is proof that God possesses them also.

As we have seen, the basis of our concept of God is this idea of a universal Life-principle that manifests itself — whether as Being or Becoming — in creation, and envelops and pervades everything, like an atmosphere of which we are unconscious until we are taken out of it. This thought is not quite enough. Consulting our own needs, we find we want something more of God than a Life-principle, himself uncaused, but who causes all that we are. The idea of a Life-principle is therefore the fabric upon which to embroider further concepts, for we have the right to think of God as representing not only the explanation of what we are but also the satisfaction of what we need. Since these needs are as numerous as mankind, and as varied as human experience, it is evident that the conceptual pattern we embroider on that fabric will be different for each individual. This is as it should be; the concept of God is a sacredly private and intimate matter, which each soul must attempt in his own way. Yet certain needs are common to us all. We may profitably consider at least two of these common needs. They are the need of recognition as individual souls or personalities, and the need of some objective or purpose to give meaning and value and direction to life.

They say that no two autumn leaves are alike. That is true of individualities. "Individual" is that which cannot be divided between two; it all belongs to one. Josiah Royce has shown that while we can classify human individualities into certain general categories, like phlegmatic, or sanguine, or nervous, we can never put our finger on the precise spiritual formula that is Abraham Lincoln and not George Washington, or that is George Washington and not Abraham Lincoln. We are conscious of each other's individualities and of our own, but the secret of our uniqueness forever eludes us. Perhaps that is what Professor A. N. Whitehead meant by saying that sooner or later each individual has to recognize the fact of his own ultimate solitariness; that in the last analysis nobody can perfectly understand us, or perfectly sympathize with us, or perfectly answer our thoughts or satisfy our needs. We are mysteries to each other, and even to ourselves.

That is a terrifying thought — that in the final analysis each one of us is alone in a cold, uncomprehending world. It is an unendurable thought. When Professor Whitehead tries to pacify that terror by saying "religion is what the individual does with his own solitariness," he gives us just the lead we want. Paul does the same service: We are "hid with Christ in God." God holds the secret of each individuality. He knows us; and, although we know in part, we shall know even as we are known. Our basic concept of God as the pervading Life-principle is not enough. What does the Life-principle know or care about individualities? What individual justice can I get in my dealings with an impersonal Life-principle? One day I put my hand in the fire from an impulse of reckless folly. Another day I put my hand in the fire to save the two-year-old who has toppled over into the fireplace. What does the Life-principle care about my motive? It burns my hand just as severely for the good motive as for the bad. There was once a good tailor in a sizable country town. He was skillful and honest. Someone asked him how he happened to set up in that town. " Eight years ago," he replied, " I spent two hours between trains in this town. I strolled through the streets, into stores, post office and library. I did not see a single man whose clothes exactly fitted him. I knew it was a ready-made-clothing town, and there was a chance for me, because I measure each customer, and give individual attention, and make the clothes that fit him." The ready-made operations of a Life-principle fit the individual no better than the ready-made clothes fit the haphazard customer. Because you are an individual, because the thought of your solitariness as an individual is unendurable, you have the right and the duty to think of God as the source and secret of all individuals, himself the Consummate Individuality, who recognizes you, understands you, makes allowances, and rewards your soul with the considerate justice that perfectly fits you. We can embroider that thought upon our basic concept of God. He is the Consummate Individuality.

Finally, without the thought of purposefulness in our concept of God, we are as lost and helpless as a great modern factory, equipped with every necessary machine, supplied with ample stocks of raw material, its belt line in full running order, its operatives each at his post, but without a single order to fill. To be able and ready to do things but not to have a single thing to do is the most dangerous condition there is. In that condition, aimlessness, like a deadly miasma, settles down on human spirits and invites every form of vice and corruption, bad habits, loose morals, extravagant pleasures, unchecked vanities and passions. Perhaps some future historian, looking back on this first half of the twentieth century from a point of rectifying perspective, will say that these two terrible wars were provoked by a cause deeper than all the surface jealousies and animosities of the times put together. They were caused by a deep-lying spiritual unrest, a fundamental despair at the heart of humanity. Civilization was getting nowhere. We had lost our headway. We were floundering about in a morass of futility. We had lost our sense of destiny. We had traversed our wilderness and reached our Promised Land, and there was nothing left for us to do but just live. The *status quo*, with all its imperfections, wrongs and injustices, was about to settle down upon us and freeze us in the economic pattern of our life as of that day. Now human hearts will put up with incredible burdens as long as they feel those burdens are only temporary and incidental to the attainment of better conditions in the not so distant future, but as soon as they realize that forward movement toward that better future has ceased, that incidental burdens are to be considered permanent, that the strained, unnatural, exhausting posture is to be maintained indefinitely, like Atlas forever holding up the heavens, then the despair comes down black and angry. Anything is better than this unendurable burden. No wonder the wars came, both of them. Human living is like riding a bicycle: you have to go on or you fall off.

What has all this to do with our concept of God? Merely this: if we have a right to consider our own fundamental spiritual needs, and to formulate our thought of God as the answer to those needs, then here is a profound and undeniable spiritual need — for an objective to enlist and control the energies within us, which nothing can imprison and which clamor for their outlet and exercise: a God of Purpose, whose spirit shall sweep like a mighty gale across the oceans of history, pick up every human heart as if it were a becalmed ship, and fill its sails, and tauten its sheets, and quiet its din of rattling blocks, and drive it along in the silence and intentness of really progressive living toward its divinely appointed haven.

Better men than we have recognized that need in our human nature, and have answered it by thinking of God as the God who works toward an end; a purposeful God; a Father who hath a business (" I must be about my Father's business "); a Father who " worketh hitherto, and I work." Other features in our concept of God may be pleasanter; none is more important. We have told ourselves that God is what we make him. In the exercise of that privilege we have taken counsel of our inclinations, and have fashioned for ourselves a pleasant God, indulgent, understanding, sympathetic, forgiving, one who will sanction the easy-going, pleasure-loving, irresponsible, self-absorbed life that seems to be fashionable just now — but we might as well get this matter straight right here: God is not what we make him. God is himself, his own wondrous and incomprehensible reality. What we strive to fashion is only a concept of God and, unless we employ the most scrupulous honesty and the most unsparing self-acquaintance we are capable of, we are wasting our time. If we are ready to consult, not our inclinations, but the incontrovertible facts of our condition, our concept of God will present him as a rather austere God, terrible in his purpose and in his intentness on that purpose; who brooks no interference and forgives no negligence; whose laws are the right methods couched in the form of mandates by which to fulfill his purpose, and which operate in our human history with a precision so inexorable that with trembling lips we whisper, " The fear of the Lord is the beginning of wisdom." Do we need a third war to tell us that? God has an end in view. Because it is his end it is holy. Good and evil derive their quality according as they serve or hinder that holy purpose. God's laws are the mandates that bid us to seek the good and avoid the evil, and if human beings want to survive there is only one way: to obey his laws, to do his right and to serve his purpose. Our concept of God is faulty and hopelessly inadequate unless we include that feature, and all that it implies — the purposefulness of God.

Now to summarize briefly: We have seen that the two considerations, what we are and what we need, are our best intimations as to the nature of God; starting with these, on the theory that the Creator must be at least all that his creation is, we must form our concept of God. This concept becomes larger as modern knowledge discovers more wonderful truths concerning creation.

Modern knowledge is the accumulated body of knowledge that has validity for us now, regardless of its age, and must include within itself the achievements of the great speculators of pre-Christian times, as well as the discoveries of the most recent scientist.

The most noticeable effect of modern knowledge is the tendency to give back certain concepts it had formerly discarded; chiefly the monistic conception of the oldest thinkers which looks upon God as the primal, all-pervading and single Life-principle.

To this basic concept we can add two more that modern knowledge once denied us, but is now ready to permit: first, that God may be thought of as the Consummate Individuality; second, that God may be thought of in terms of Purpose.

Professor Kirsopp Lake said that the task of the modern theologian is to devise a theology that shall satisfy the soul without disgusting the mind. That is to say, the function of modern knowledge is not to formulate but to censor our concept of God; where it goes against the grain of man's reason, to forbid it by its disgust; and where it keeps within reasonable limits, to allow it by its acquiescence. We can see how true this is in the present instance, for about all the effect modern knowledge, as of this day, has on the concept of God is that it has decided to withhold some of the disgust it has formerly felt, and permit the soul to conceive of God in ways that not so many years ago it would have condemned as being intellectually disgusting. We are very grateful to modern knowledge.

8

MAN'S DESTINY IN ETERNITY

Willard L. Sperry

WILLARD L. SPERRY has been dean of the Harvard Divinity School and professor of Practical Theology since 1922. In the past he served as dean of the National Council on Religion in Higher Education, and as a trustee of Vassar College. Dr. Sperry has written *Strangers and Pilgrims, What We Mean by Religion, Rebuilding Our World* and *Religion in America*.

8 *Willard L. Sperry*

MAN'S DESTINY IN ETERNITY[1]

*T*HERE IS CURRENT among us a familiar phrase about "those who profess and call themselves Christians."

One of the traditional duties required of us by our religion is that of self-examination and, if need be, of self-criticism. In the discharge of this duty we often find ourselves asking by what right, or on what basis, we call ourselves "Christians." Various conventional answers have been given, but none of them are today entirely convincing, at least to those of us who are not content with the theological conventions of the past.

We might say that we call ourselves Christians because we belong to a church. But this answer has never been accepted as wholly satisfactory. According to theology the visible church is a mixed sort of affair; true Christians are those who belong to the invisible church, and the membership of the invisible church is known only to God.

We might say that we are Christians because we believe a given creed or a certain set of theological propositions. This is a risky account of the matter, since no theology persists unmodified, and all theologies are in constant process of change. The formal theology we hold today may be outmoded tomorrow.

Few of us, or none, would have the effrontery to say that we can call ourselves Christians because our characters coincide

[1] Delivered at Lancaster, Pennsylvania, as the Garvin Lecture for 1947, under the title, "The Immortality of Man."

with the moral ideals proposed in the teaching of Jesus. Those ideals represent the counsel of perfection, and, so far from being perfect, we know ourselves to be sadly imperfect. Only a hypocrite or a Pharisee would say that he is morally good enough to be called a Christian.

Culturally we have been members of an old and widespread society in the Western World, conventionally known as " Christendom." In that sense of the word we are Christians rather than Mohammedans or Hindus. But this designation is little more than a historical platitude. What is more serious, the onetime integrity of the Western World has been gravely impaired in these last years, so that Christendom is by no means as integrated a cultural fact as it was once supposed to be.

In short, it is not as easy as it might seem to find a decent and defensible warrant for calling ourselves Christians. The nearest I have ever been able to come to it might be put in some such way as this: " I believe myself to be standing in an unbroken organic succession of human experience which has its moral and spiritual origins in the Bible. This succession I feel to be a living thing, as in a family, and not a mechanical thing. To use a classic phrase from the past, my Christianity has been 'begotten, not made.' I did not fabricate it for myself. No one made it for me, in imitation of a past model. This temper and manner of life which I call my Christianity is a life principle. I wish to continue in it, and to pass it on to those who come after me. I have no wish to break with it, whatever problems of faith and conduct it may present to me. I want to live with it and by it and to perpetuate it."

This is vague, but I am certain that some will understand. I will not labor the point, or try to defend it. I could cite evidence from thinkers of the first rank in defense of some such theory. (This idea is, I believe, what is meant by the great doctrine of the " Communion of Saints.") I venture to let the statement stand in my own rather intimate and informal words.

If any defense of this account of Christianity be needed, it may be had from the simple observation that something of the sort is what has actually happened in history. At least two great theologians of our time, Father George Tyrrell and Dean William Ralph Inge, have defended the proposition that there is not and never has been any such entity as " Christianity " as a " thing-in-itself." Christianity, they say, was from the first, and remains to this day, a quality of life, a spirit, a mode of thinking and feeling and acting, which can be infused into any formal secular system that it may chance upon. The thirteenth chapter of I Corinthians may, thus, be taken as a description, even a definition, of Christianity. Christianity is a matter of faith and hope and love. These are tempers of the soul rather than dogmas. As long as they survive, no matter in what form, there we have the Christian religion as a living thing.

This interpretation of Christianity allows of, if it does not indeed require, a flexibility of mind that is in danger of emptying great words of their meaning. From his own standpoint the Biblical fundamentalist is quite right in saying that we liberals and modernists are not Christians. He would deny his faith were he to admit that we may be called Christians. And most of us have known reflective moments — in reading the New Testament, for instance — when we feel with overwhelming force the difference between the mental world of that time and that of our own time, the radical departure human thought has made from the premises that governed the thinking of that distant age. These differences concern the doctrine of God, our conception of the universe round about us, the nature of man, the processes of history and the like. The thinking of the first century took place within a compact and comfortable framework. Our thinking in the twentieth century takes place within a vast framework, so extended that we can hardly imagine its limits and its impersonality. When this contrast weighs heavily upon us, we are at times doubtful whether Christianity, as it was first conceived, has at its command today enough vitality to allow for restatement in the now accepted terms of our own thought. Will not the restatement result in so different a body of doctrine that the original word " Christianity " will have lost both its content and its validity? Such is the conclusion to which many intelligent persons are being driven in our day. They can no longer " profess and call themselves Christians."

I have presented this situation in some detail because it puts to us the most acute aspect of our subject, the immortality of the human soul. The Christian religion in the strict sense begins not with the teaching of Jesus but with certain convictions about him which his followers proposed to their world. Technically, one cannot call Jesus a Christian. He was the occasion and the warrant for Christianity; without him there would have been no Christianity. But, in so far as the Christian religion has been not so much the religion *of* Jesus as a religion *about* Jesus, he could not have been formally included in the movement that was to bear his name.

Whatever else the disciples thought and knew about Jesus, they knew that he had risen from the dead. Even those of us who find it difficult to accept the letter of the Gospel accounts of Easter agree that the disciples were experiencing a spiritual reality rather than a ghostly illusion. The Christian religion was launched on the world as a confident assurance of immortality. All the books of the New Testament ring the changes on this conviction. Take, for instance, not as an exception but as a typical statement of this common conviction, the majestic words at the beginning of the First Epistle General of Peter: " Blessed be the God and Father of our Lord Jesus Christ, which according to his abundant mercy hath begotten us again unto a lively hope by the resurrection of Jesus Christ from the dead, to an inheritance incorruptible, and undefiled, and that fadeth not away."

It would be unfair to the preaching of the first Christian spokesmen to say that the hope of immortality, transformed by the resurrection of Christ into a certainty, was the only article of their faith. But there is no denying that it was essential; they were, at this point, witnessing to a fact rather than advancing a theory which invited speculation. The Jewish world, which lay behind the Gospel, had come only slowly and tentatively to a belief in immortality and was, in the time of Jesus, still divided on the matter. The Pharisees affirmed it; the Sadducees denied it. The world of classical antiquity, by which primitive Christianity was environed, may have held vague views as to the possibility, or even the probability, of the life hereafter; but these views lacked both clarity and conviction.

There is no doubt that the appeal of Christianity rested from the outset in no small part upon its absolute assurance in this regard. Christ had risen from the dead. Believers in Christ would rise with him. What had happened to him — and there was no doubt as to the event — was what was to happen to them when their time came. One feels throughout the New Testament what might be called a tremendously heightened vitality. Here is life, life abundant, life eternal. With this assurance of immortal life came also a great serenity. Nothing that could happen to us here, not any or all of the vicissitudes of human experience, could separate us from Christ. Faith in immortality was so confident that the whole question of life after death was moved from the area of uncertainty into the area of certainty. The issue was, as the lawyers have it, not justiciable.

What was true with that first Christian generation remained true for centuries thereafter. Many of the major doctrines of Christianity, those that concern the nature of deity, the person of Christ, the nature of man, sin, forgiveness, salvation, the church, the sacraments — all of these have been, over the centuries, subjects of controversy, occasions for heresies and even for persecutions and martyrdoms. But no historic Christian sect has ever denied the doctrine of man's immortality.

Yet now, and for reasons by no means easy to identify, this

central and perhaps most characteristic article of the Christian faith over all the past centuries has moved back from the area of certainty to that of uncertainty — or if not to that of uncertainty then to that of studied neglect. It may be true that in the more orthodox and conservative religious circles of our day faith in immortality persists confident and unimpaired. It may further be true that in more liberal circles this faith is still privately cherished by single individuals. But, given our American Protestant culture as a whole and its dominant concerns, this earthly life of three- or fourscore years is our center of interest, and the next life counts for little in our everyday thought.

I put it to you, therefore, that there is no single article of the traditional Christian faith less confidently affirmed today than this about immortality, and none so generally neglected or doubted. At this point the contrast between the traditional Christianity of the past and the conventional Christianity of today is so marked that one often wonders whether so much of our modern Christianity as is basically skeptical on the matter has a right to use the word " Christian " as a form of self-designation. A religion that is purely this-worldly, and confessedly indifferent to any next world, has departed so far from the original that common decency in the use of words might suggest the impropriety, if not the outright falsehood, of designating such a religion as " Christian." There is a point beyond which the theories of accommodation and restatement cannot be carried with good conscience. The man who thinks that Jesus, a Galilean carpenter who lived for some thirty years, is now dead and gone forever, save for what is called his " immortality in history " — and that this is to be the fate of all the rest of us — can hardly be called a Christian in the historic sense of the term.

This contrast between the faith of the fathers and the skepticism or perplexity of our own time is such that we cannot help wondering why men today find it natural to doubt what their forebears believed as a matter of course. Why do we no longer take for granted that faith of the fathers? Why do we constantly and deliberately confine our conception of religion to this world, to the neglect of any and all other worlds?

Two or three answers suggest themselves at once. Our greatly perfected understanding of human physiology has undoubtedly tended to incline us to regard consciousness, and thus self-consciousness — the mind, the spirit, the soul — as functions of the brain, wholly dependent upon that double handful of gray matter for their very being. We sometimes talk about the soul as though it were a quantum that can be weighed and measured, like the other data of science; but no man hath seen a soul at any time. If it exists, it is an elusive aspect of our mortal life, providing of itself no guarantee of its own immortality.

Furthermore, those of us who hold a faith in some world of the spirit cannot help being sobered and challenged by the apparent close dependence of rationality, morality, character and the like upon the condition of a given human brain. When we learn what brain injuries can do to induce madness and moral degeneracy, and what operations can do to restore sanity and virtue, we cannot help wondering whether all that is meant by the worlds of reason and virtue are not merely by-products of physiological processes, having no independent reality of their own.

It is a commonplace to say that we live in a materialistic age. This materialism has, to a certain extent, invaded the central shrine or citadel of personality. We give more thought to the body, its care, its gratification, its appearance, than our fathers have given for many generations past. But, what is perhaps more serious, we accord it a primacy in experience, which by contrast tends to depreciate all that is meant by the life of the mind, the life of the soul. In short the " physiological " premises for a confident faith in immortality are by no means as universal as once they were.

A second reason for our difficulties with the idea of immortality is the substitution of the Copernican for the Ptolemaic astronomy. The old cosmology made heaven a not improbable or unimaginable place in the skies overhead. The Bible says, again and again, that now this hero and now that " went up into heaven." The Copernican astronomy has made all such language impossible, save in the most figurative usage. Pascal looked out three hundred years ago on what has come to be called " the expanding universe " and said: " The eternal silence of these infinite spaces terrifies me." That is what any thoughtful man feels as he thinks of astronomical space and time. Rudyard Kipling pictured the situation when he said of the wandering soul of Tomlinson: " The wind that blew between the worlds, it cut him to the bone."

This case has been stated with dramatic fidelity to the modern mind in a superb passage of one of George Tyrrell's works:

If our astronomy has in some way enlarged, it has also impoverished our notion of the heavens. It has given us quantitative mysteries in exchange for qualitative. As the mind travels endlessly into space it meets only with more orbs and systems of orbs in their millions, an infinite monotony of matter and motion. But never does it strike against some boundary wall of the universe beyond which God keeps an eternal Sabbath in a new order of existence. The heaven that lay behind the blue curtain of the sky, whence by night God hung out his silver lamps to shine upon the earth, was a far deeper symbol of the eternal home, than the cold and shelterless deserts of astronomical space. [2]

I need not labor this case.

In the third place, the rise and spread of the social gospel in the nineteenth century shifted much of the ethical concern of the Christian religion from the rewards and punishments of the life hereafter to the vindication of righteousness here and now, on this earth and in our lifetime. The theory that virtue should be its own reward was always defensible and has be-

---

[2] George Tyrrell, *Lex Credendi* (London, 1906), pp. 109-110.

come increasingly fashionable. After the death and burial of his little son, Thomas Henry Huxley wrote a letter to Charles Kingsley. He said that the officiating minister read at the graveside the words of St. Paul, " If the dead rise not, let us eat · and drink, for tomorrow we die." Wrote Huxley:

I cannot tell you how inexpressibly they shocked me. I could have laughed with scorn. What! because I am face to face with an irreparable loss, because I have given back to the source from whence it came the cause of a great happiness, still retaining through all my life the blessings which have sprung and will spring from that cause, I am to renounce my manhood, and howling grovel in bestiality? [3]

Most moderns have shared Huxley's position.

Beyond this conviction that the good things of life are their own reward and need no supplement to vindicate or to fulfill them, there arose a century ago, and there is still widespread today, the conviction that the hope of heaven has been deliberately held out to sufferers in this world, to prevent their protesting against the injustices they endure on earth. The classic instance in our American tradition is the prominence given to the idea of heaven in the Negro spirituals. Slaves had nothing to hope for here beyond their chains. Release was to be had only with death and the passage over Jordan. There is, I fear, no doubt that godly slaveowners, not unwilling to make the best of both worlds, fostered among their slaves this convenient aspect of the Christian religion. When she was in New Orleans in the 1830's, Harriet Martineau noticed that advertisements in the papers occasionally stressed the bargain to be had in a lot of pious Negroes being offered in the slave market. They would give no trouble here and now.

Likewise there was an uneasy suspicion, a generation ago, that, in certain industrial areas where employees and towns

---

[3] Leonard Huxley, *Life and Letters of Thomas Henry Huxley* (New York, 1902), I, 237.

were all under company control and where labor conditions and pay were far from just, the management encouraged and perhaps even subsidized preachers who dwelt on the hope of heaven, to the exclusion of prophets who might have talked about decent housing and a fair livelihood here on earth. Certain types of unethical big business would seem to have counted the hope of immortality as a financial asset. Hence, among the more ethically impatient spokesmen for the social gospel, the whole idea of immortality was deliberately laid aside in the interest of some account of life on earth that should be a more probable forecourt of heaven than was the current social order. Heaven and immortality were not denied. They were simply postponed, until we could get this earth a little more tidied up morally. In any case we were not to allow the hope of heaven, held out to unfortunate victims of social injustice, to be used as a subtle warrant for perpetuating economic injustices for the profit of ourselves or anyone else. Nineteenth-century liberal Christianity went out for a here-and-now righteousness, and for punishments and rewards that could be experienced on the spot.

As a result of these three most patent considerations, which have for some years impinged upon the traditional Christian doctrine of the immortality of the soul, that idea has become vague and remote in the minds of most liberal Christians, and, indeed, in the minds of many of the more conservative and orthodox Christians. The truth is that the average American Christian, whether orthodox or liberal, thinks very little about the life hereafter; and, whatever his creed may expect of him, the thought of that life has little influence upon his conduct. He is not deterred from doing wrong by the fear of hell, or prompted to do right by the hope of heaven. He is rather like that Saracen woman whom St. Louis once met on the streets of a Levantine city. She had a jug of water in one hand and a lighted torch in the other hand. The crusader asked her what she was proposing to do with them. She said that she was going to put out the fires of hell and burn up the joys of heaven, that men might love God for his own sake.

The traditional faith of the Christian in a life hereafter is suffering not from a frontal attack of outright skepticism, but rather from neglect. Dean Inge once said that God cannot be very real to a person who devotes no more than three minutes a day to the thought of him. So we might say that the immortality of the soul cannot be very real to one who thinks of it only occasionally.

As for these three deterrents I have mentioned, a word may be said. The scientific view of the world is probably not as grossly materialistic as it was fifty years ago. What might be called the leaden materialism of yesterday has given way to a theory of energy as the truth of the physical universe. It is a misuse of words to call such energy "spiritual," but at least the universe as a whole is construed to be much more vital and less lifeless than it once was thought to be. Furthermore, while we do not question the influence of matter, in the form of the brain, upon our thoughts, we do acknowledge today to a degree not anticipated by our predecessors the converse influence of mind upon matter. Ideas and emotions have a great influence upon the fortunes of the body.

I have no wisdom to add to what has been called "the astronomical intimidation" now meted out to man's onetime thought of a provincial heaven. The where and how of another life remain an inscrutable mystery. As to the ethical preoccupation of our generation with the vindication of righteousness here and now, at the expense of possible future rewards and punishments, I am inclined to say that this preoccupation is to our moral credit, rather than otherwise. The idea of immortality ought not to be used as a shrewd device for the perpetuation of injustices here on earth.

But the net result of these and other factors bearing on the situation is the widespread lack of confidence in the immortality of man, and the resultant perplexity and skepticism, that are commonplaces in circles such as our own. When Henry Thoreau was dying, a pious friend asked him what he thought about the next world. Thoreau looked up with a wan smile and said, " One world at a time, brother, one world at a time." That story has given no little reassurance to the skeptics of our day. I have cited Thomas Huxley. By his own direction three lines from a poem written by his wife were inscribed on his tombstone:

> Be not afraid, ye waiting hearts that weep;
> For still He giveth His beloved sleep,
> And if an endless sleep He wills, so best. [4]

Many a modern can subscribe with entire good heart and good conscience to such a sentiment. The idea of total annihilation for oneself is by no means repugnant; it is not even incredible. To go to sleep and never to wake up is not an intolerable prospect. Even if one expects to waken, the idea of some prolonged mid-rest is welcome. Thus, there is in an old German cemetery a stone that says: " When thou callest me, Lord Christ, I will arise. But first let me rest a little for I am very weary."

Contrariwise, the human mind can never be made perfect in its skepticism. As Robert Browning has it, once we settle this sort of issue in our mind, and dismiss all idea of a life hereafter as being a proven impossibility,

> Just when we are safest, there's a sunset-touch,
> A fancy from a flower-bell, some one's death,
> A chorus-ending from Euripides,—
> And that's enough for fifty hopes and fears
> As old and new at once as nature's self,
> To rap and knock and enter in our soul,
> Take hands and dance there, a fantastic ring,
> Round the ancient idol on his base again,—
> The grand Perhaps! [5]

[4] Huxley, *Life*, II, 426.

[5] Robert Browning, *Poetical Works* (London, 1888), IV, 245.

A sophisticated friend of mine put our case in reverse when he said: " Most of the men whom I know aren't afraid there isn't any immortality, they're afraid there is." If you wish to state the case positively, but in its lowest terms, you might cite a wry remark that Huxley made in a letter to John Morley:

It is a curious thing that I find my dislike to the thought of extinction increasing as I get older and nearer the goal. . . . I had sooner be in hell a good deal — at any rate in one of the upper circles, where the climate and the company are not too trying.[6]

That reflection is, after all, a commonplace. It is when we are young and strong and healthy that we can contemplate with detachment the prospect of total annihilation, primarily because that idea has no plausibility at such a time. The human mind is, ultimately, unable to think of itself as nonexistent, and it is from this psychological fact that much of what might be called our native inclination to believe in a life hereafter has its origins.

Be these several considerations as they may, we are all of us confronted today with two facts: one of these facts is part of the constant experience of the race; the other is an occasional experience. We are, in the first instance, confronted with the fact of death as it invades our own homes. Death comes intimately, imperiously and at times inscrutably. There is no getting away from it. The conventions forbid our parading our grief, and, indeed, require us to keep our sorrow to ourselves, lest our friends and the community round about be unduly disquieted. But as we go through this recurring experience, as we hear the words, " earth to earth, ashes to ashes, dust to dust," we cannot help asking: " Is that the whole story; is that the end?"

This is, perhaps, the moment to enter our instinctive protest against the statement, so often made, that the hope of immortality is unworthy of a generous-minded soul because it is

* Huxley, *Life,* II, 67.

basically selfish. Our thought of immortality is far more altruistic than selfish. It has been said that there are, in the presence of death, two prospects we cannot endure: one, that our beloved lives no more; the other, that the great and good of the world are "perished as though they had never been." We can endure with equanimity the thought that we may not live again; we cannot endure the thought that our loved ones and our heroes are dead forever.

Then, beyond what might be called this recurring, intimate experience of death, there has been for the last thirty years the appalling toll of corporate death in our wider world as the result of two wars and the consequences of those wars. On February 23, 1855, at the time of the Crimean War, John Bright stood up in the House of Commons and made one of the most memorable speeches of the last century. He said:

An uneasy feeling exists as to news which may arrive by the very next mail from the East. . . . Many homes in England in which there now exists a fond hope that the distant one may return — many such homes may be rendered desolate when the next mail shall arrive. *The Angel of Death has been abroad throughout the land; you may almost hear the beating of his wings.*[1]

What was true then has been more widely and tragically true in our day. Early in the First World War, Sigmund Freud wrote a little treatise called *War and Death*. He said that the war was proving how thin and precarious the veneer of civilization has been over our savage and primitive selves. Then he went on to say that at no point has modern, supposedly cultured man been more dishonest and more sentimental than in the presence of the fact of bodily death. We disguise it from ourselves, we avoid contact with it, we are afraid of it because we do not understand it, and we shirk it because we have no answer to it. He went on to add, therefore, that whatever else

[1] George Macaulay Trevelyan, *The Life of John Bright* (Boston, 1913), pp. 243-244.

war might do it would once more domesticate the dead body of a man in the common mind as a familiar and inevitable fact.

All of us, in the face of the untimely dying of millions of young men in our day and the wholly undeserved deaths of plain folk — little children, harmless civilians, the aged — have had to give to the fact of death sober meditation which may not have been required of our fathers in more quiet times. Have these last years merely lighted a foolish generation the way to dusty death, and nothing more? In short we are back again in the book of Job: " If a man die, shall he live again?"

In coming to final grips with these reflections, as they pass through our minds, I wish to make one distinction. It is possible to discuss the problem of the immortality of man on what might be called a purely humanistic basis; that is, to project our human experience out into infinite time and space, and more particularly to try to get, by means of the still imperfect science of psychical research — if that venture can be said to have achieved the status of a science — assurance that the human personality survives death. This result is to be had through the technique of séances, trances and mediums. It invokes no God as its warrant or its goal.

No one would wish to discourage experiments of this sort. These are not, however, transactions in which a layman should be encouraged to dabble. A prominent member of the British Society for Psychical Research once said to me that one must go into psychical research off the deep end, or leave it alone. One should not paddle in it up to the knees. It is an area where deception has been frequent and where the peril of self-deception is even greater. Meanwhile, for the purposes of this discussion I venture to point out that, while religion may welcome such confirmation as is given to its hope of immortality from this source, it does not rest its case upon such findings, and on the whole tends to be indifferent to them. The religious man thinks of the life immortal as being the object of faith, while psychical research is trying to make it the subject of scientifically assured knowledge. The two approaches are not merely distinct — they are different. You may have noticed, for example, the antipathy of the Bible for all sorcerers, witches and the like. The witch of Endor called back the shade of Samuel to serve Saul in his extremity. Anyone who reads the story must feel not merely its ghostliness, but also its suggestion that something dangerous and even wrong was being done. The woman was reluctant to do what Saul asked of her; the spirit of Samuel protests at having been invoked. The whole transaction is felt to be out of bounds.

The reason for this constant disallowance of what we should now call séances is based upon a deep and instinctive feeling that, wherever the dead may be and whatever their lot may be, it is not their destiny to be at our beck and call. The reference back from some other world to this world is felt to be a reversal of values. The whole Biblical premise for the idea of immortality is found in the story in II Samuel of the death of the child that the wife of Uriah bore to David. "Now he is dead," says David, "can I bring him back again? I shall go to him, but he shall not return to me."

There is no one in what we might call a religious relation to the idea of immortality who does not take these words as his point of departure. The hope that we may bring our dead back to us is vain; any attempt to conceive of heaven, and of the life of those that are in heaven, as existing primarily to render service to this earth and to us who are still on earth is religiously mistaken. The memory of our dead is dear to us. We often feel them strangely near to us, their example inspires us. All this is true. But the attempt to call them back and to keep them at our beck and call is mistaken. If there be any immortality at all, they must have their own life with its own concerns, more real than the concerns of our life here. The idea, not that they shall return to us, but that we shall go on to them, is constant throughout the Bible. The religious reference is, therefore, always from this life to the next life, from earth to heaven. In your moments of loneliness or perplexity you may go to the witch of Endor, but you must not assume that the impulse that prompts you to do so is an act of faith or that she is a minister of religion.

Not only is this so, but the Bible, as the idea of immortality begins to emerge in the Old Testament and finds its full and unequivocal statement in the New Testament, seems to suggest that dying is a matter not so much of going into some strange land as of going home. Josiah Royce, the late Harvard philosopher, used to say that Christianity had given man his " principal glimpse of the homeland of the human soul." One of the medieval mystics put it in another and even more picturesque way. He said that God is at home and it is we who are in the far country.

Much of the Christian symbolism of death makes use of this metaphor. The world of the spirit, the homeland of the human soul, is, to cite Francis Thompson's term, " No Strange Land." This conviction has crept into much of the nontheological, but nonetheless truly religious, verse of our time. You will remember Robert Louis Stevenson's " Requiem ":

> Under the wide and starry sky
> Dig the grave and let me lie;
> Glad did I live and gladly die,
>   And I laid me down with a will.

> This be the verse you grave for me:
> *Here he lies where he longed to be;*
> *Home is the sailor, home from sea,*
>   *And the hunter home from the hill.* [8]

I am inclined to think that what might be called a purely naturalistic approach to this simple idea is to be had from a recovery of the lost sense of the inevitableness of death and, indeed, of its essential rightness, together with a feeling of reposefulness in the thought of the dust returning to its dust. Our modern lives are so sophisticated and unnatural that most

---

[8] Robert Louis Stevenson, *Works* (London, 1912), XIV, 86.

of us have lost, entirely, a feeling for the fitness of the committal of the body to the earth. I do not think that Wordsworth felt sad when he wrote his lines to Lucy, or that he intended us to feel sad. He felt only a great serenity in the fact he recorded:

> No motion has she now, no force;
> She neither hears nor sees;
> Rolled round in earth's diurnal course,
> With rocks, and stones, and trees. [9]

Now these moods or metaphors about one's return to mother earth, one's going home, are the subsoil out of which the mature Christian doctrine of immortality springs. For, in some very real sense, man is overheard saying at the hour of death, " I will arise and go to my Father." Once again the Old Testament anticipates what is to be the full faith of the New Testament. The most skeptical and yet the most realistic book of the Old Testament is Ecclesiastes. But it is in this book that we find what sometimes seems to be the first and the last of all the statements one can make about our subject: " Then shall the dust return to the earth as it was: and the spirit shall return unto God who gave it."

The New Testament gives more mature and intimate accounts of the event; it does not alter the basic idea. The account of the life hereafter is, at times, that of the unnumbered multitude of just men made perfect standing in the presence of God. It is at other times that of our passing on into one of the many mansions in a Father's house. " I leave the world," runs the saying of Christ in John's Gospel, " and go to the Father. . . . I ascend unto my Father, and your Father; and to my God and your God."

As far as religion is concerned, and the Christian religion in particular, we might well rest our case there. In the hour of sorrow we say, " The Lord hath given and the Lord hath taken away, blessed be the name of the Lord." In the hour of

---

[9] William Wordsworth, *Complete Poetical Works* (Boston, 1904), p. 113.

our own dying we say, " Into thy hands I commend my spirit." These are acts of faith. For religion they are all that is necessary. What is more than this is little else than idle speculation.

In the biography of Frederick Temple, Archbishop of Canterbury, it is told that one of his clergy, troubled over the doctrine of immortality, appealed for help on the matter. The Archbishop listened patiently, but made only few rather casual comments. The other man broke out, in some impatience, " My lord, have *you* never had any of these troubles? Don't *you* ever feel the mystery of that other life?" The Archbishop replied, " Yes, I think I know what you mean. But I believe so entirely that God is my Father, and that he loves me, and that he will make me perfectly happy in the other life, that I never worry myself over what that life will be." " I remember thinking," the clergyman goes on to say, " here is one of the biggest men in England living in the same simple faith that supports the humblest Christian washerwoman — belief in God's love. The answer did more to help me than anything else he said." [10]

One of the simplest and most familiar statements of this faith is found in Whittier's lines on *The Eternal Goodness:*

> I know not what the future hath
> Of marvel or surprise,
> Assured alone that life and death
> His mercy underlies. . . .
>
> I know not where His islands lift
> Their fronded palms in air;
> I only know I cannot drift
> Beyond His love and care. . . .
>
> And Thou, O Lord! by whom are seen
> Thy creatures as they be,
> Forgive me if too close I lean
> My human heart on Thee! [11]

[10] E. G. Sandford, editor, *Memoirs of Archbishop Temple* (London, 1906), II, 655.

[11] John Greenleaf Whittier, *Writings* (Boston, 1912), II, 270-271.

So construed, belief in immortality is, in a sense, a secondary rather than a primary article of our faith. It is a corollary of a prior belief in God.

A scientific humanism may debate the possibility of immortal life on its own merits. The humanist is quite within his own rights in so doing. The purely humanistic attitude toward a future life has seldom had a more accurate or tender expression than is to be found in the famous lines that the dying emperor Hadrian composed and addressed to his soul:

> *Animula, vagula, blandula, . . .*
>
> O blithe little soul, thou, flitting away,
> Guest and comrade of this my clay,
> Whither now goest thou, to what place
> Bare and ghastly and without grace?
> Nor, as thy wont was, joke and play.[12]

Here we have our humanity shorn of all sense of commerce or correspondence with the universe around. The soul is alone with itself, homeless and uncompanioned. But one who believes in God believes also that in him we live and move and have our being. Our immortality is conditioned by that fact.

Therefore, for most of us, the problem of immortality must be referred back to the antecedent problem of the being and nature of God.

If our traditional beliefs about heaven have proved hard to hold in the face of modern science, so have our conventional beliefs about God. An increasing number of serious persons are driven to the conclusion that we are confronted by what one of the great scientists of the last century called " the passionless impersonality of the unknown and the unknowable." He goes on to say that he is not able to find the slightest evidence that this great unknown behind the phenomena of the universe stands to us in the relation of a Father. The traditional doctrine

---

[12] *The Scriptores Historiæ Augustæ*, translated by David Magie (New York, 1922), I, 79.

of the Fatherhood of God is today, more than ever, a bold affirmation of faith, rather than an obvious inference from the facts.

Let me put the case for this belief in a rather crude way. Suppose that the human race were to be wiped off this planet by some cosmic catastrophe, and suppose that other persons like ourselves, on other planets, were to suffer a like fate at the same time — would the process that we know as thought have ceased in the universe? Difficult as it is to imagine what such a process or principle may be, it is even more difficult to believe that the only thoughtfulness there is in the total scheme of things is that which goes on in our human minds. We speak of the discoveries of science, and that is the right word. The major truths are truths that we do not create but find. They represent facts and transactions in the natural order which exist in their own right, waiting there to be matched by our minds. So it is that Wordsworth has a phrase of ascription to God which says, " O Thou, who art an eternity of thought." Much that we observe, it is true, seems to us irrational, morally indifferent and even cruel. Nevertheless, when we are oppressed by the perplexities that always attend a positive faith, it is well to face the reverse side of the shield. If untroubled faith is hard to come by, thoroughgoing skepticism is just as hard to hold, perhaps harder.

In any case, once we have said that we believe there is in the total scheme of things " an eternity of thought," we have the foundation for a doctrine of God. This is the affirmation with which John's Gospel opens. The term " Word " used there is, of course, taken from Greek philosophy; it connotes the whole idea of a planned world and of thoughtfulness shot through all things. The Christian religion requires that this thoughtfulness shall not be restricted to reasoning or reflection. It shall be supplemented by feeling and construed as love. It shall be moral, seeking good rather than evil. All this must be picturesquely stated in the terms of human experience and at the consequent risk of anthropomorphism: that is, the risk of making God in our own image and of thinking of him as such an one as ourselves. But there is no escape from this risk. We have to think in these terms or not at all. We need only to remind ourselves constantly that we are using metaphors and symbols, not fashioning precise definitions.

Once you have believed in this eternity of thought, and believed in it as loving and good, then the idea of the immortality of man is not irrational, it is not incredible. Indeed, mysterious as it all is, it seems far more probable than otherwise. The life of the mind is, as we have said, conditioned by the fact of the body. But on the whole most of us will agree that the life of thought, with the emotion and the will that accompany it, is our most real life; and that of all the processes in which we are involved, thinking — and particularly thinking in the terms that our religion proposes for the conduct of life — is life at its best.

For myself, I find it increasingly difficult to divorce human thought from the " eternity of thought." The former is framed within the latter. And so I find it hard to believe that human minds and hearts and wills can come to the maturity and the splendor that the race achieves so constantly, only to be snuffed out and thus to end abruptly in nothingness. It seems more probable that the process that initiated these lives of ours must make provision for their conservation.

I can only venture in conclusion two or three private ideas as to possible ways and means of this immortality. I do so with some reluctance, because of all this we have no knowledge, and our ideas should probably be described as creations of fancy rather than of imagination.

As to the whereabouts of heaven and the locale for immortality, we can say absolutely nothing. We know nothing of pure spirit and we simply cannot venture any theories as to the dwelling place for an immortal soul. That is why so many persons have to fall back on the doctrine of the resurrection of the body. That at least is something that can be pictured, although few of us now hold literally to this idea.

What is most at stake is the probability or the assurance that personality shall persist, and the test case is the survival of self-consciousness and of memory. Can we still go on saying " I " of a consecutive experience? Are we going to know one another again, shall we recognize one another? More particularly, can hearts separated by death be reunited, in some fresh immediacy? We have it in the words of Christ that in that life there will be no marrying or giving in marriage. Plainly no such particular types of human relationship will be resumed in their earthly form. But if we admit that all the more intimate relationships of life, and in particular the emotions that attend them, are the ways and means by which we come really to know one another and to arrive at what is so often called " deathless love " — then our thought of immortality must carry with it the confidence that in some manner, which we cannot anticipate, we shall recognize one another, love one another and go on together with our common life. Any conception of immortality that reduces it to impersonality deprives it of most of its meaning. A growing knowledge of God will normally be matched by a growing knowledge of one another.

Having said this, I must go on to say that a distinction should probably be made between the idea of individual immortality and that of personal immortality. Of those two words, " individual " is the lesser and " personal " the greater. One is more and more impressed by what might be called the impermanence of one's own individuality. That individuality is always in process of being enlarged or supplemented. So much is this so that the individual you were twenty years ago would conceive of the individual you now are as almost a plural being. We would not wish the individual we shall be at the moment of death to be arrested at that point and perpetuated through all eternity in those terms. The immortality we hope for is that of a limited individual forever in the process of becoming more of a person. Kirsopp Lake once said that immortality will probably prove to be one's chance to learn to say " we " instead of " I." What he meant, I take it, is that immortality will enlarge our individuality at the same time that it makes our social ties stronger and more intimate. But one need not suppose that in this process the continuity of self-consciousness is lost. The " we " of tomorrow will still be aware of the " I " of yesterday.

The hope of immortality matured only slowly in the Old Testament. It was the result of long reflection upon the character of God and the operations of his righteousness. In particular the sufferings of Israel during the exile and the failure of the Messianic Age to come speedily to pass fostered the conviction that the righteous dead must be raised at the last time to share in the Messianic Kingdom. It did not seem fair to shut them out of that consummation because they lived too soon. Life here and now is certainly grossly unfair to countless persons, if we try to equate their character with their earthly status. We can only say that, being woven into the social web of humanity, many individuals enjoy undeserved good and others must endure undeserved evil. The ledgers of society probably balance in the long run; the day books of the single man seldom balance.

One cannot help feeling — looking back over the last thirty years and remembering the tide of youth that has passed out of this life before it had really put the cup to its lips and known our human experience in something like its entirety — that, if there be any fairness in the total scheme of things, that scheme owes them something. If all these are " perished as though they had never been " we cannot suppress a feeling of rebellion and resentment as well as of sorrow. The memory of them and their example certainly ought to make us better, but that fact hardly compensates them for their sacrifice. I am not laboring this point, but merely emphasizing that considerations such as this give to our subject an urgency which in more tranquil times it sometimes lacks.

One further reflection -- or, perhaps more accurately, one more fancy. Is it possible to save what was once intended by the doctrine of heaven at the same time that we dispense with the antithetical idea of hell? The two terms have usually traveled together. The terrifying pictures of hell painted by Jonathan Edwards in his lurid sentences are no longer plausible. Dante's hell was incredibly somber, Milton's hell was magnificent but cruel. Most of us are through with that doctrine. Perhaps the fact that we are through with it has in some measure contributed to our skepticism as to heaven. If we cannot have heaven save at the price of hell, then we will forego the hope of heaven for the sake of ridding humanity of its naked fear of hell. (I am, of course, using these words pictorially.)

But, if we dispense with hell, does this mean that if we believe in the life hereafter everybody will go to heaven? Some Christians think so. In this matter I subscribe to Mark Rutherford's appraisal of mankind: " I never, hardly, see a pure breed either of goat or sheep. I never see anybody who deserves to go straight to heaven or who deserves to go straight to hell." The older theory, that one's eternal destiny was decided and determined in these threescore years and ten, and signed and sealed at death, is so improbable as to be incredible. It has been said that the occupation of eternity will be the task of realizing the commandment of Jesus, " Be ye therefore perfect, even as your Father which is in heaven is perfect." The successful continuation of the moral struggle, the perfecting of self-discipline, do give credible content to the idea of the life hereafter as against what has been called the " sad, sunny idleness of heaven."

But what about those persons who, as it were, seem to be headed in the wrong direction and stubbornly insistent on going that way? At the time when she retired from the presidency of Radcliffe College, Miss Ada Comstock said that, looking back over her life, she realized that she had made one serious mistake: she had underestimated the positiveness of evil. We have had to witness a great deal of coldly rationalized, relentlessly pursued, positive evil in the last few years. What about the destiny of the men who conceived and executed it? Well, the mercy of God is infinite, the patience of God untiring, and the most evil of men may experience some " irresistible grace." But I have never been able to see why a man who is deliberately set upon committing spiritual suicide should not be allowed to do so. All that you and I mean by life, by the good life, shrinks, dwindles and falls away when evil is made the good and goal of living. I cannot see why the destiny of the undeviating sinner may not be, ought not to be, naked nothingness. Hell, so construed, would be merely zero.

It is said that the objection to this idea of the possible self-annihilation of the evil man is to be found in the reflection that under such circumstances the only one who suffers is God. The man himself knows nothing, feels nothing; he is blacked out at some moral vanishing point. But through all eternity God will have to realize that at one of his ventures with mankind he has failed. The idea that God should fail at anything and have to admit that he has failed is to many minds intolerable. I have never been able to feel the force of this objection. God took that chance when he gave us our genuine moral freedom, and he was prepared for his own reflective pain as well as for his joy.

Finally, I beg you not to take these concluding reflections too seriously. They are flights of fancy, not articles of faith. I have ventured to take them simply because no one of us can avoid thinking about such matters, once he faces the mystery of the life hereafter. I would rest my argument upon the thesis proposed midway in the lecture, that if we believe in God we may also go on to believe that we cannot drift beyond his love and care. All this, perhaps, can be given point in a single swift sentence of Emerson's in his essay " The Over-Soul." The destiny of the human soul, he is saying, cannot be thought of apart from its communion with the Over-Soul. This is the way he puts it: "The moment the doctrine of immortality is separately taught, man is already fallen."

One of the most classic statements of this conviction is that to be found in St. Augustine's *Confessions:* "Blessed is he who loves Thee, and his friend in Thee, and his enemy for Thee. For he alone loses no one dear to him, to whom all are dear in Him Who never can be lost." [13] We reach those whom we have loved and lost awhile, not so much directly, as by way of God.

If we wish to recover something of the great confidence of the first Christians in the life hereafter, I can do no better than to cite some words of George Matheson, the blind poet and hymn writer:

Son of Man, whenever I doubt of life, I think of Thee. Nothing is so impossible as that Thou shouldest be dead. I can imagine the hills to dissolve in vapor and the stars to melt in smoke, and the rivers to empty themselves in sheer exhaustion; but I feel no limit in Thee. Thou never growest old to me. Last century is old, last year is an obsolete fashion, but Thou art not obsolete. Thou art abreast of all the centuries. I have never come up with Thee, modern as I am. . . . Nothing is so impossible as that Thou shouldest be dead. [14]

---

[13] *The Confessions of St. Augustine*, Book IV, ch. ix.

[14] Quoted in W. L. Sperry's *The Disciplines of Liberty* (New Haven, 1921), p. 19.

9

THE IDEA OF GOD AS AFFECTED BY MODERN KNOWLEDGE

F. S. C. Northrop

F. S. C. NORTHROP, Sterling professor of philosophy and law at Yale University, is the author of *Science and First Principles*, *The Meeting of East and West* and *The Logic of the Sciences and the Humanities*. He is a member of the executive committee of the National Conference on Science, Philosophy and Religion.

9 *F. S. C. Northrop*

THE IDEA OF GOD AS AFFECTED BY MODERN KNOWLEDGE[1]

*J*T IS OBVIOUSLY necessary to restrict oneself to but one portion of so tremendous a topic. Roughly there are two major aspects of modern knowledge which are relevant: one, the specific content of this knowledge; the other, its generic character as specified by the methods by means of which this content is obtained. Historically, in both the Occident and the Orient the character of man's idea of God has been determined as much by the way of knowing as by what is known. Hence it is quite appropriate in the present inquiry to concentrate in greater part on the bearing upon the idea of God of the character of modern knowledge in so far as this character is specified by the methods by means of which it is obtained. Also, in considering the character of modern knowledge, we shall begin with that form of it which has received the greatest unanimity of assent, and which has most characterized the modern Western world, while at the same time being the one type of knowledge which contemporary Orientals most want to obtain from the West. I refer to Western scientific knowledge.

Modern Western scientific knowledge has one very remarkable characteristic. It is the most practical knowledge the world has ever witnessed, and at the same time the most theoretical. The atomic bomb, for example, was made possible by a mathe-

[1]Delivered at Lancaster, Pennsylvania, as the Garvin Lecture for 1948.

matical formula relating energy to mass by way of an absolute constant *c,* where *c* is the velocity of light. Albert Einstein came upon this matter-energy equation when he pursued the logical consequences of his special theory of relativity. The latter theory in turn arose as a result of Einstein's successful attempt to clarify the relation between matter, its motion, and space and time. Only a mind such as Einstein's, interested primarily not in practical gadgets such as the atomic bomb, but in the most abstract, theoretical problems at the basis of modern physics and philosophy, would ever have discovered the special theory of relativity, from which the mass-energy equation — upon which the atomic bomb rests — derives.

Consider another example, a commonplace one in homes throughout the world today — the radio. This very practical instrument is one of the initially unforeseen end products of a most theoretical type of inquiry pursued by the English mathematical physicist Clerk Maxwell in the nineteenth century. It started with the very imaginative and almost esoteric assumption of Maxwell's predecessor Michael Faraday, that nature is to be conceived as a field filled with lines or " tubes " of force, rather than as an aggregate of discontinuous, discrete atoms or particles of matter. Faraday's notion was ridiculed by the authoritative scientists of his time. Maxwell took up the idea, however, and gave it a mathematical formulation. When it was thus formulated, he was able to deduce the then-known, experimentally verified laws of electricity and magnetism. In this manner, Faraday's imaginative theory was indirectly and experimentally confirmed.

Note the logic of the method of modern mathematical physics as illustrated by Faraday and Maxwell. After many observations of electrical or magnetic phenomena — such as the distribution of iron filings on a sheet of paper near, but not in contact with, a magnet — there was suggested to Faraday's imagination the hypothesis that the apparently empty space between the paper with its iron filings and the magnet is not really empty but is instead part of a continuous field embracing all nature and filled with lines or " tubes " of force of which the behavior of the iron filings and the magnet are the expression.

Certainly this is a bold hypothesis, going far beyond anything that anyone can directly observe; so far in fact that, as we have noted, Faraday was ridiculed by the scientists of his time. Nevertheless Maxwell was able to show that Faraday's bold leap of the imagination is correct. How, one may well ask, is the scientist thus able to establish the existence of an electromagnetic field embracing all nature, such as Faraday's imagination envisaged, which cannot be directly seen? Maxwell gives us the answer. This answer throws light on the logic of modern physics and the indirect method of confirmation which it prescribes for attaining trustworthy knowledge.

Maxwell began by assuming tentatively Faraday's imaginative hypothesis. He then asked what follows if it is true. To this end, he applied formal logic to its assumptions or postulates, thereby deducing its logical consequences. But, to deduce logical consequences from any theory, the assumptions of the theory must be very precise. Faraday's imaginative notion of a field of force filled with lines or " tubes " of force ending in termini which Faraday called " sources and sinks," while suggestive, is not sufficiently exact. Hence, before Maxwell could determine the logical consequences of Faraday's imaginative hypothesis, he had to become even more theoretical and abstract than was Faraday. In other words, Maxwell's first move was to give Faraday's concrete images of a field with its tubes of force an abstract mathematical formulation. Then and only then could concrete consequences capable of being put to test in a physicist's laboratory be rigorously deduced from Faraday's vividly imaginative theory. When this abstract mathematical formulation was achieved by Maxwell, he had no difficulty in deriving all the then-known, experimentally verified laws of electricity and magnetism.

Nevertheless, this indirect experimental confirmation did not establish Faraday's theory. For there existed at the time another mathematically formulated theory, resting on the assumption that nature is a system of particles related by forces acting upon one another at a distance. Furthermore, this particle-physics theory developed by André Marie Ampère also accounted for all the experimentally verified laws of electricity and magnetism. Moreover, it had the additional merit of using the same theoretical assumptions for electricity and magnetism that Newton had shown to be required in mechanics. Consequently, notwithstanding Maxwell's demonstration that Faraday's field physics can account for all the facts in electricity and magnetism, it did not win the support of other scientists because Ampère's electromagnetic theory could do the same without departing from the assumptions of Newton's mechanics.

Nonetheless Maxwell pursued Faraday's theory farther. He noted that, in his initial mathematical formulation of it, the law of the conservation of energy was not satisfied. Since all evidence points to the validity of this law, Maxwell concluded that he must modify his mathematical formulation of Faraday's theory in such a way that the law of the conservation of energy holds. When this was done, a remarkable constant c definable experimentally appeared in the mathematical electromagnetic equations. This constant had mathematically the dimensions of a velocity, thereby prescribing a wave propagation in the electromagnetic field with the velocity c, which is 186,000 miles per second *in vacuo*. This remarkable theoretical deduction and discovery gave Faraday and Maxwell's electromagnetic field-physics theory its triumph over Ampère's Newtonian particle-physics theory. Even those scientists who had ridiculed Faraday were eventually persuaded.

The considerations leading to the persuasion merit further specification. The velocity of 186,000 miles per second *in vacuo* happened also to be the experimentally known value of the velocity of light. Thus light was for the first time connected with electricity and magnetism and shown to be a special case of electromagnetic propagations in the electromagnetic field. Immediately, certain discoveries made fifty years previous to Maxwell by Thomas Young and Augustin Jean Fresnel came to mind. At the opening of the nineteenth century, Young and Fresnel had experimentally demonstrated the interference phenomenon associated with converging rays of light, which is explicable only if light is conceived as a wave propagation rather than an emission of discrete particles. These experimental findings revealed by Young and Fresnel were in fact the sole factors in physics for which the traditional particle physics of Newton and Ampère could not account. Consequently, when Maxwell derived the wave propagation of light with its specific velocity c from Faraday's assumptions, he accounted for facts that no previous theory could explain. Young and Fresnel's experimental findings were now intelligible. Faraday's theory was uniquely confirmed.

But more than this even was to come from Maxwell's theoretical mathematical formulation and pursuit of Faraday's imaginative theory. Optical-wave propagations, we have just noted, were revealed thereby to be a special case of electromagnetic propagations. This suggested to Maxwell that there could be many different wave lengths with their accompanying waves moving in the electromagnetic field with the velocity c, other than the several different wave lengths of the different colors of visible light. In fact, Maxwell noted that it would be a quite arbitrary restriction of the wave propagation — a restriction unwarranted by the assumptions of the theory — if wave lengths both longer and shorter than those of visible light do not exist in nature.

The question naturally arose whether it is possible by experimental means to detect electromagnetic propagations in nature with these other wave lengths. Suffice it to say that a German physicist, Heinrich Rudolph Hertz, derived from

Maxwell's equations rules for the construction of an experimental apparatus which must operationally detect these theoretically predicted wave lengths if they exist. He constructed the theoretically prescribed apparatus and performed the theoretically prescribed operations. The directly inspectable correlates of the novel predicted wave lengths were found to be there. It is these Hertzian electromagnetic waves which now exhibit their most practical presence in radio and radar.

Truly, modern scientific knowledge has a remarkable character. While the most practical the world has ever possessed, it is at the same time the most intangible, speculative and abstract. It appears that the more theoretical we are the more practical we become.

Modern scientific knowledge as exhibited in the foregoing analysis has one other characteristic. It reveals nature to us as possessing a component designated only by theory indirectly verified experimentally through its deductive logical consequences. Moreover, nature as thus known to us by theory indirectly and uniquely verified experimentally is quite different from nature as directly observed. It is important to have a name for this theoretically known component of nature. It seems appropriate, following the usage of my books *The Meeting of East and West* (1946) and *The Logic of the Sciences and of the Humanities* (1947), to call it *the theoretic component.*

Modern scientific knowledge, in making us aware of this theoretic component in nature, at the same time exhibits man and the mind of man as the imaginative, creative, mathematically and logically formal and rationalistic kind of thing which can know nature in this way. Thus modern scientific knowledge throws as much light on the nature of man and man's creative mental capacity as it does on the nature of the physical universe. In fact, it is in contemporary mathematical physics that we find the most unequivocal evidence of the creative imagination of man and of his rational capacity to formulate ideas abstractly and to carry through rigorous, logical deductions. In short, the theoretic component is revealed by modern scientific knowledge to be a real component not only of physical but also of human nature. Modern mathematics demonstrates that man in the theoretic component of his nature, when he achieves the scientific theory necessary to give the most practical results, is a rational animal.

The extent to which this is true of contemporary knowledge in mathematical physics merits further elucidation. We have noted how Faraday resorted to the empirical imagination to arrive at the idea of the electromagnetic field which lies at the basis of the science of electricity, magnetism and optics. This field is not given by images derived directly through the senses. It is given, instead, by images posited by the creative imagination. Recently, however, all such images have had to be dropped as being inadequate representations of nature. The creative, purely intellectual imagination has had to replace the creative sensuous imagination.

The following considerations have brought scientists to this conclusion. The atoms of Newton's particle physics as well as the waves of Faraday's field physics have been mentioned. Recent experimental evidence indicates, however, that both images break down. Scientific objects that the imagination would envisage as particles behave in certain experiments as if they were waves; conversely, scientific objects that the imagination envisages as waves behave in certain experiments as if they were particles. In other words, any attempt to obtain a single conception of nature in terms of the images of the creative sensuous imagination breaks down before the experimental findings. The facts simply are not what should be the case were nature what the creative sensuous imagination postulates.

As a consequence, contemporary quantum mechanics, for example, in its conception of nature, has had to resort to the creative formal or intellectual imagination alone. To use the language of Socrates in his account of the passage from scientific hypotheses of the sensuous imagination to " the idea of the good," at the end of Book VI of Plato's *Republic*, one proceeds " making no use of images." Einstein's theory of relativity illustrates this same dropping of images. According to the latter theory, nature is a single four-dimensional continuum with field properties defined in terms of the formal, logical properties of relations. The creative sensuous imagination cannot envisage a continuum of more than three dimensions. Again, therefore, the creative, purely formal or intellectual imagination must be resorted to. Nature as known in the small in quantum mechanics, and in the large in the theory of relativity, is a theoretically and intellectually known world.

Similarly the scientific mind that knows nature in this way is a mind with a creative imagination which can work purely intellectually without images. Never has there been a more unequivocal demonstration of the theoretic component in nature and of the creative, theoretic and purely intellectual nature of the human mind equal to that given in the discovery, formulation and verification of the theories of contemporary mathematical physics. Yet no knowledge has ever been more practical in its fruitfulness.

Nature, as known by this science, is a theoretically and intellectually known world, and man, as the formulator, discoverer and verifier of such trustworthy and effective knowledge, thereby demonstrates himself to be a truly creative and intellectual creature.

Yet this is but one half of the story. For contemporary scientific knowledge is not merely theoretical, formal and extremely intellectual, devoid of sensuous images; it is also empirically verified. Empirical verification means that it has its roots in sensuous immediacy as well as in the abstract forms proposed creatively by the intellect. To grasp its complete character, therefore, we must examine with care what is given with empirical immediacy.

What is the character of that which we immediately apprehend? No question, it would seem, is easier to answer. Yet curiously enough there is no question that is more frequently answered erroneously.

The usual reply is that one immediately apprehends tables, chairs, and other persons as external objects and one's own personal self as a determinate, persistent, substantial entity. Nothing at first thought seems more obvious. The slightest careful examination, however, soon shows this supposedly obvious supposition to be false.

Consider first the table conceived as an external, material object. As such it is three-dimensional with right-angled corners. It also possesses a back side as real as the side that confronts us directly. Clearly one does not see its back side; one can at best see only the side before one. But, it may be said, one can walk around the table and see the back side. But then one will not see the side that is now before one. It is only by carrying the image of the present front side with one in memory while one walks around the table, and then combining it with the image obtained at the end of one's journey and with a large number of other images received on the way, that one gets the idea of the many sides of the table together simultaneously. Furthermore, what puts them together? Clearly it is not sight or observation. Observation merely gives the one image after the other image; it does not give all the images simultaneously so joined together as to give a single three-dimensional table with right-angled corners. Clearly, then, if we possess, as we do, knowledge of a single three-dimensional table with right-angled corners, this common-sense knowledge requires a creative act of the imagination; like Faraday's experimental field, it is not given by mere observation or immediate apprehension alone.

The same is true of one's observed self. When one looks at one's self by means of introspection, one apprehends merely an associated set of different feelings and other sensuous qualities — warmth, colors, irritations and so on — succeeding one another in time, and different from moment to moment. One does not apprehend a determinate, constant, identical self, present beneath these sensations and even persisting during sleep through the night when obviously one is not looking at one's self. This does not mean that one's beliefs in a persistent self, or in tables with right-angled corners existing as external, material objects, are erroneous. It means merely that such beliefs, like beliefs in Faraday's electromagnetic field or Einstein's four-dimensional space-time continuum, are not given by observation or immediate apprehension alone but depend on imagination and the constructive power of the intellect also. It means, furthermore, that the correct answer to the question concerning what we directly observe leaves us with something very important — but much less than, and quite different from, the beliefs of common-sense knowledge.

What then is the character of that which we directly observe or apprehend? Our analysis has already given the answer. We immediately apprehend not material tables and chairs, but images and sensuous qualities — colors, flavors, fragrances, pains, pleasures. These are felt, fuzzy-edged aesthetic qualities; they are not the three-dimensional, sharp-edged material objects of common sense. In other words, they are the kind of things with which the modernistic, impressionistic artist works, rather than the common-sense material objects and substantial persons with which the ordinary man in daily life is continually concerned. For this reason it is appropriate, again following the usage in my *Meeting of East and West* and *Logic of the Sciences and of the Humanities*, to call the empirically immediate component in nature and man *the aesthetic component*.

One caution with respect to it must be noted. It is not merely the sequence of felt, sensuous qualities afore-mentioned, but also the all-embracing field or continuum of immediacy within which they come and go. In other words, the aesthetic component of nature and man is the immediately apprehended and felt aesthetic continuum with its transitory sensuous differentiations or qualities.

This directly observed, immediately felt and apprehended continuum must not be confused with the theoretically known continuum or field of Faraday's electromagnetics or Einstein's four-dimensional space-time. Hence the adjectives "aesthetic" and "theoretic" to distinguish the directly verified continuum given with immediacy from the theoretically designated and indirectly verified continuum of mathematical physics.

We are now able to give a complete account of the character of contemporary scientific knowledge of nature and of man. It involves an intellectually and theoretically known part which we call the theoretic component, and an immediately felt and apprehended part which we term the aesthetic component. Without the theoretic component, the theoretical character of contemporary scientific knowledge would not be present; without the aesthetic component, the empirical verification of this scientific knowledge would not be possible. In short, contemporary scientific knowledge tells us that both nature as known and man as its knower are ultimately the kind of thing of which intellect on the one hand, and sensuous emotive feeling on the other, are made and which they alone can designate.

Moreover, an analysis of the relation between these two components of man and nature, carried through in Chapter XII of *The Meeting of East and West,* has demonstrated that neither component is illusory or the mere appearance of the other. They both are irreducible the one to the other, and hence ontologically as well as epistemologically ultimate. It was shown also in that book that the four intuitive religions of the Far East — Brahmanism, Buddhism, Confucianism and Taoism — identify their idea of God with the indeterminate, immortal, intuitively given factor in the aesthetic component of nature and man; and that the three theistic religions of the West and Middle East — Judaism, Christianity and Mohammedanism — identify the idea of God with the determinate, relational, invariant or immortal factor in the theoretic component of nature and man. Since contemporary scientific knowledge embraces both the aesthetic and the theoretic components as ultimate, real and irreducible roots of nature and human nature, it appears that an idea of God which is abreast of contemporary knowledge must enlarge the traditional concepts of God in the two major civilizations of the world to include in the single, complete divine nature the intuitive, indeterminate, aesthetic component of the intuitive religions of the Far East and the theoretic, determinate component of the theistic religions of the West and the Middle East.

We are living in an atomic age in which the failure to bring international deeds under the control of a single world law may mean the death of civilization. There are reasons [2] for believing that, before we can hope to obtain the agreement in the political acts of men necessary for the creation of an effective world law, there must be agreement in the basic beliefs from which these acts stem. Thus the way to a single world religion, richer in its idea of the divine nature than any of the many existent competing religions, may well be a necessary accompaniment of the achievement of world law and the preservation of the hard and slowly won cultural institutions and values of mankind.

If this enrichment of the many present religions of the world by their transformation into one world religion is to be achieved as prescribed by the light of modern knowledge, one additional advance is necessary. Intimations of a theoretic component in nature and man, which is ultimate and immortal and hence divine, came early in the history of the Western world. The importance of these early theistic premonitions, as recorded in the ancient bibles and sacred books, can hardly be over-

[2] See Eugen Ehrlich's evidence that any codified law must have its basis in "the living law," in his *Fundamental Principles of the Sociology of Law* (Cambridge, Mass., 1936); also Professor Pitirim A. Sorokin's *The Reconstruction of Humanity* (Boston, 1948).

emphasized. Nonetheless, the content of this theoretic component of divinity as thus initially conceived was usually excessively tribal, provincial and anthropomorphic on the one hand, or extremely ambiguous on the other. Consequently, the story of Western religious thought is the story of the continuous reformulation of its content in the light of new and further knowledge. The present conception of this content is no exception to this rule; it, too, cannot be that of yesterday. Hence, an adequate idea of the theoretic component of divinity must fill that component in with content derived from today's rather than yesterday's empirically verified and theoretically formulated knowledge.

Furthermore, this contemporary reformulation, following the afore-mentioned extremely intellectual and theoretic character of contemporary scientific knowledge, will be much more intellectual and rationalistic in its emphasis than is the traditional, modern Western religious doctrine. In this respect it will be more like medieval Arabian Mohammedanism and Judaism and Augustinian Platonic — rather than Thomistic Aristotelian — Roman Catholicism. The contemporary content, however, will give expression to the reformatory spirit of contemporary Turkish Mohammedanism, early prophetic Judaism and the initial modern Protestantism.

It appears, therefore, that contemporary knowledge entails two enlargements and enrichments of the traditional idea of God. First, the Oriental intuition of the divine as all-embracing, indeterminate, immediate feeling must be combined with the Western theistic conception of the deity as a doctrinately designated, determinate being. Second, the Western theistic contribution to this more complete, richer, truly universal world religion must be re-expressed in more completely non-sensuous, intellectual form with contemporary content.

The result will be a religion which places a greater emphasis upon passion, feeling and intuitive aesthetic sensitivity on the one hand, and upon reason, doctrine and intellect on the other hand, than does any one of the many existing religions. It is to be emphasized especially that this is not the tepid, watered-down common denominator of the many existing religions of the world that is usually suggested as a world religion; instead, the existing, separate religions are each made more passionate and intense in their own particular genius. The emotional love of God and the intellectual love of God are each maximized and then merged.

INDEX